AZ-104: Microsoft Azure Administrator

Practice Questions

Second Edition

www.ipspecialist.net

Document Control

Proposal Name	:	Microsoft Azure Administrator - Practice Questions
Document Edition	:	Second Edition
Document Release Date	:	2nd May 2023
Reference	:	AZ-104

Registered in England and Wales
Company Registration No: 10883539
Registration Office at: Office 32, 19-21 Crawford Street, London W1H 1PJ, United Kingdom
www.ipspecialist.net

Feedback:
If you have any comments regarding the quality of this book, or otherwise alter it to better suit your needs, you can contact us through email at info@ipspecialist.net
Please make sure to include the book's title and ISBN in your message.

About IPSpecialist

IPSPECIALIST LTD. IS COMMITTED TO EXCELLENCE AND DEDICATED TO YOUR SUCCESS.

Our philosophy is to treat our customers like family. We want you to succeed and are willing to do everything possible to help you make it happen. We have the proof to back up our claims. We strive to accelerate billions of careers with great courses, accessibility, and affordability. We believe that continuous learning and knowledge evolution are the most important things to keep re-skilling and up-skilling the world.

Planning and creating a specific goal is where IPSpecialist helps. We can create a career track that suits your visions as well as develop the competencies you need to become a professional Network Engineer. Based on the career track you choose, we can also assist you with the execution and evaluation of your proficiency level, as they are customized to fit your specific goals.

We help you STAND OUT from the crowd through our detailed IP training content packages.

Course Features:

- Self-Paced Learning
    - Learn at your own pace and in your own time
- Covers Complete Exam Blueprint
    - Prep for the exam with confidence
- Case Study Based Learning
    - Relate the content with real-life scenarios
- Subscriptions that Suits You
    - Get more and pay less with IPS subscriptions
- Career Advisory Services
    - Let the industry experts plan your career journey
- Virtual Labs to test your skills
    - With IPS vRacks, you can evaluate your exam preparations
- Practice Questions
    - Practice questions to measure your preparation standards
- On Request Digital Certification
    - On request digital certification from IPSpecialist LTD.

About the Authors:

This book has been compiled with the help of multiple professional engineers. These engineers specialize in different fields e.g., Networking, Security, Cloud, Big Data, IoT, etc. Each engineer develops content in its specialized field that is compiled to form a comprehensive certification guide.

About the Technical Reviewers:

Nouman Ahmed Khan

AWS-Architect, CCDE, CCIEX5 (RandS, SP, Security, DC, Wireless), CISSP, CISA, CISM is a Solution Architect working with a major telecommunication provider in Qatar. He works with enterprises, mega-projects, and service providers to help them select the best-fit technology solutions. He also works closely as a consultant to understand customer business processes and helps select an appropriate technology strategy to support business goals. He has more than 18 years of experience working in Pakistan/Middle-East and UK. He holds a Bachelor of Engineering Degree from NED University, Pakistan, and M.Sc. in Computer Networks from the UK.

Abubakar Saeed

Abubakar Saeed has more than twenty-five years of experience, Managing, Consulting, Designing, and implementing large-scale technology projects, extensive experience heading ISP operations, solutions integration, heading Product Development, Presales, and Solution Design. Emphasizing adhering to Project timelines and delivering as per customer expectations, he always leads the project in the right direction with his innovative ideas and excellent management.

Dr. Fahad Abdali

Dr. Fahad Abdali is a seasoned leader with extensive experience managing and growing software development teams in high-growth start-ups. He is a business entrepreneur with more than 18 years of experience in management and marketing. He holds a Bachelor's Degree from NED University of Engineering and Technology and a Doctor of Philosophy (Ph.D.) from the University of Karachi.

Mehwish Jawed

Mehwish Jawed is working as a Senior Research Analyst. She holds a Master's and Bachelors of Engineering degree in Telecommunication Engineering from NED University of Engineering and Technology. She also worked under the supervision of HEC Approved supervisor. She has more than three published papers, including both conference and journal papers. She has a great knowledge of TWDM Passive Optical Network (PON). She also worked as a Project Engineer, Robotic Trainer in a private institute and has research skills in the field of communication networks. She has both technical knowledge and industry-sounding information, which she utilizes effectively when needed. She also has expertise in cloud platforms, such as AWS, GCP, Oracle, and Microsoft Azure.

Free Resources

For Free Resources: Please visit our website and register to access your desired Resources Or contact us at: helpdesk@ipspecialist.net

Career Report: This report is a step-by-step guide for a novice who wants to develop his/her career in the field of computer networks. It answers the following queries:

- What are the current scenarios and future prospects?
- Is this industry moving toward saturation, or are new opportunities knocking at the door?
- What will the monetary benefits be?
- Why get certified?
- How to plan, and when will I complete the certifications if I start today?
- Is there any career track that I can follow to accomplish the specialization level?

Furthermore, this guide provides a comprehensive career path towards being a specialist in networking and highlights the tracks needed to obtain certification.

IPS Personalized Technical Support for Customers: Good customer service means helping customers efficiently, and in a friendly manner. It is essential to be able to handle issues for customers and do your best to ensure they are satisfied. Providing good service is one of the most important things that can set our business apart from others.

Excellent customer service will attract more customers and attain maximum customer retention.

IPS offers personalized TECH support to its customers to provide better value for money. If you have any queries related to technology and labs, you can simply ask our technical team for assistance via Live Chat or Email.

Our Products

Study Guides

IPSpecialist Study Guides are the ideal guides to developing the hands-on skills necessary to pass the exam. Our workbooks cover the official exam blueprint and explain the technology with real-life case study-based labs. The content covered in each workbook consists of individually focused technology topics presented in an easy-to-follow, goal-oriented, step-by-step approach. Every scenario features detailed breakdowns and thorough verifications to help you completely understand the task and associated technology.

We extensively used mind maps in our workbooks to visually explain the technology. Our workbooks have become a widely used tool to learn and remember information effectively.

Practice Questions

IP Specialists' Practice Questions are dedicatedly designed from a certification exam perspective. The collection of these questions from our Study Guides is prepared to keep the exam blueprint in mind, covering not only important but necessary topics. It is an ideal document to practice and revise your certification.

Exam Cram

Our Exam Cram notes are a concise bundling of condensed notes of the complete exam blueprint. It is an ideal and handy document to help you remember the most important technology concepts related to the certification exam.

Hands-on Labs

IPSpecialist Hands-on Labs are the fastest and easiest way to learn real-world use cases. These labs are carefully designed to prepare you for the certification exams and your next job role. Whether you are starting to learn a technology or solving a real-world scenario, our labs will help you learn the core concepts in no time.

IPSpecialist self-paced labs were designed by subject matter experts and provided an opportunity to use products in a variety of pre-designed scenarios and common use cases, giving you hands-on practice in a simulated environment to help you gain confidence. You have the flexibility to choose from topics and products about which you want to learn more.

Companion Guide

Companion Guides are portable desk guides for the IPSpecialist course materials that users (students, professionals, and experts) can access at any time and from any location. Companion Guides are intended to supplement online course material by assisting users in concentrating on key ideas and planning their study time for quizzes and examinations.

Microsoft Certifications

Microsoft Azure Certifications are industry-recognized credentials that validate your technical Cloud skills and expertise while assisting your career growth. These are one of the most valuable IT certifications since Azure has established an overwhelming growth rate in the public cloud market. Even with several tough competitors such as Amazon Web Services, Google Cloud Engine, and Rackspace, Azure will be the dominant public cloud platform today, with an astounding collection of proprietary services that continues to grow.

In this certification, we will discuss cloud concepts where we will learn the core benefits of using Azure, like high availability, scalability, etc. We will talk about the Azure Architecture in which cloud resources are put together to work at best; Azure Compute, where you will learn how to run applications in Azure; Networking, in which the discussion is on how Azure resources communicate with each other; Storage, where you put all of your data and have different ways of storing it. We will also cover databases used for data storage, their efficient retrieval as per demand, and ensuring that the users have the right access to the resources. Also, we will counter some complex scenarios with their solutions. We will have discussions on important topics like; Security, which makes Azure the best secure choice for your applications and functions; Privacy, Compliance, and Trust that make sure services ensure privacy and how you stay compliant with standards. As well as, pricing in Azure to stay ahead on cost.

AZ-900 is the first certification of Microsoft Azure, the foundational certificate in Azure. After this certification, you can prove to the world that you are proficient and have the credibility to reach the highest point of your professional life.

Value of Azure Certifications

Microsoft emphasizes sound conceptual knowledge of its entire platform and hands-on experience with the Azure infrastructure and its many unique and complex components and services.

For Individuals

- Demonstrate your expertise in designing, deploying, and operating highly available, cost-effective, and secured applications on Microsoft Azure.
- Gain recognition and visibility of your proven skills and proficiency with Azure.
- Earn tangible benefits such as access to the Microsoft Certified Community, getting invited to Microsoft Certification Appreciation Receptions and Lounges, obtaining Microsoft Certification Practice Exam Voucher and Digital Badge for certification validation, and Microsoft Certified Logo usage.

- Foster credibility with your employer and peers.

For Employers

- Identify skilled professionals to lead IT initiatives with Cloud technologies.
- To implement your workloads and projects on the Azure platform, reduce risks and costs.
- Increase customer satisfaction.

Types of Certifications

Role-based Certification

- Fundamental - Validates overall understanding of the Azure Cloud.
- Associate- Technical role-based certifications. No pre-requisite is required.
- Expert- Highest level technical role-based certification.

About Microsoft Certified: Microsoft Azure Administrator

Exam Questions	Case study, short answer, repeated answer, MCQs
Number of Questions	40-60
Time to Complete	120 minutes
Exam Fee	165 USD

The Microsoft Certified: Candidates for this exam should have subject matter expertise in implementing, managing and monitoring an organization's Microsoft Azure environment. Responsibilities for this role include implementing, managing, and monitoring identity, governance, storage, compute, and virtual networks in a cloud environment, plus provision, size, monitor, and adjust resources when needed. An Azure administrator often serves as part of a larger team dedicated to implementing an organization's cloud infrastructure. A candidate for this exam should have at least six months of hands-on experience administering Azure, along with a strong understanding of core Azure services, Azure workloads, security, and governance. In addition, this role should have experience using PowerShell, Azure CLI, Azure portal, and Azure Resource Manager templates.

This exam measures your ability to accomplish the following technical tasks:

- Manage Azure identities and governance (15–20%)

- Implement and manage storage (15–20%)
- Deploy and manage Azure compute resources (20–25%)
- Configure and manage virtual networking (20-25%)
- Monitor and maintain Azure resources (10–15%)

Recommended Knowledge

- Manage Azure Active Directory (Azure AD) objects
- Manage role-based access control (RBAC)
- Manage subscriptions and governance
- Secure storage
- Manage storage
- Configure Azure files and Azure Blob Storage
- Automate deployment of virtual machines (VMs) by using Azure Resource Manager templates
- Configure VMs
- Create and configure containers
- Create and configure Azure App Service
- Implement and manage virtual networking
- Secure access to virtual networks
- Configure load balancing
- Monitor and troubleshoot virtual networking
- Integrate an on-premises network with an Azure virtual network
- Monitor resources by using Azure Monitor
- Implement backup and recovery

All the required information is included in this technology workbook.

	Domain	Percentage
Domain 1	Manage Azure identities and governance	15-20%
Domain 2	Implement and manage storage	15-20%
Domain 3	Deploy and manage Azure compute resources	20-25%
Domain 4	Configure and manage virtual networking	20-25%
Domain 5	Monitor and maintain Azure resources	10-15%

Practice Questions

1. You are a company's Azure administrator. A custom role based on the Virtual Machine Contributor position must be created. The following PowerShell script must be completed.

```
$ipsrole = [SLOT 1] "Virtual Machine Contributor"
$ipsrole.Id = $null
$ipsrole.Name = "Virtual Machine Reader"
$ipsrole.Description = "Read permissions for virtual machines."
$ipsrole.Actions.Clear()
$ipsrole.Actions.Add("Microsoft.Storage/*/read")
$ipsrole.Actions.Add("Microsoft.Network/*/read")
$ipsrole.Actions.Add("Microsoft.Compute/*/read")
$ipsrole.AssignableScopes.Clear()
$ipsrole.AssignableScopes.Add("/subscriptions/00230400-0500-0440-0440-005550000000")
[SLOT 2] -Role $ipsrole
```

Which of the following would come in SLOT 1?

A. New-AzRoleDefinition
B. Set-AzRoleDefinition
C. Get-AzRoleDefinition
D. Create-AzRoleDefinition

2. A company has the following virtual networks defined in Azure.

Name	Address space
ips-network1	10.1.0.0/16
ips-network2	10.2.0.0/16

The following virtual machines have been defined as well.

Name	Network
ipsvm1	ips-network1
ipsvm2	ips-network2

The appropriate peering connections between ips-network1 and ips-network2 have been established. The virtual machines' firewalls have been adjusted to enable ICMP traffic. Yet, no traffic seems to pass between the virtual computers when a ping request is made.
Which of the following methods can be used to identify the problem?

A. Application Insights
B. IP Flow Verify
C. Azure Security Center
D. Azure Advisor

3. A company has an Azure subscription that has the resources in the following table.

Name	Type
rg-ips	Resource Group
st-ips	Azure Storage account
syncips	Azure File Sync

A file share named docs is part of the st-ips storage account. 1000 files can be shared in one document.
The files in the file sharing must be synchronized with an on-premises server named ipsserver. To meet this demand, which of the following would you need to implement? Choose three responses from the list below.

A. Create a sync group
B. Register ipsserver
C. Download an automation script
D. Create a container instance
E. Install the Azure File Sync agent on ipsserver

4. A corporation intends to move data out of its Azure Storage account via the Azure Import/Export service. When defining the Azure Export job, which of the following services could be used?

A. File storage
B. BLOB storage
C. Table storage
D. Queue storage

5. Your company has set up a storage account in Azure, as shown below.

Resource group (change) ipspecialist-rg	Performance/Access tier Standard/Hot
Status Primary: Available	Replication Locally-redundant storage (LRS)
Location UK South	Account kind StorageV2 (general purpose v2)
Subscription (change) Pay-As-You-Go	
Subscription ID baaa99b3-1d19-4c5e-90e1-39d55de5fc6e	
Tags (change) Click here to add tags	

Only IP addresses in the range 51.107.2.0 to 51.107.2.255 should be allowed to connect to the storage account. Which of the following sections of the storage account would you alter to satisfy this requirement?

A. Advanced security
B. Firewall and virtual networks
C. Lifecycle Management
D. Soft Delete

6. An Azure Virtual Machine has been set up by a corporation. The team member trying to connect to the virtual machine is having trouble. The following is a sample from the Virtual Machine's Networking section.

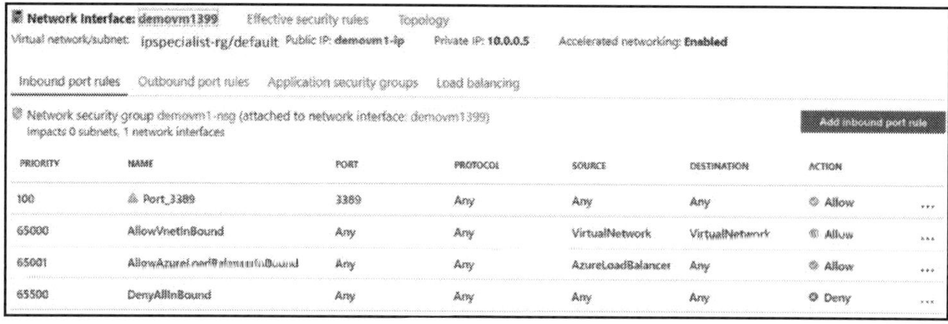

Network Interface: demovm1399 Effective security rules Topology
Virtual network/subnet: ipspecialist-rg/default Public IP: demovm1-ip Private IP: 10.0.0.5 Accelerated networking: Enabled

Inbound port rules Outbound port rules Application security groups Load balancing

Network security group demovm1-nsg (attached to network interface: demovm1399)
Impacts 0 subnets, 1 network interfaces

Add inbound port rule

PRIORITY	NAME	PORT	PROTOCOL	SOURCE	DESTINATION	ACTION
100	Port_3389	3389	Any	Any	Any	Allow
65000	AllowVnetInBound	Any	Any	VirtualNetwork	VirtualNetwork	Allow
65001	AllowAzureLoadBalancerInBound	Any	Any	AzureLoadBalancer	Any	Allow
65500	DenyAllInBound	Any	Any	Any	Any	Deny

To ensure that the team member may connect to the Virtual Machine, which of the following must be done?

A. Delete the Rule "Port_3389"
B. Delete the Rule "DenyAllInBound"

C. Start the Virtual Machine
D. Add a rule to the Outbound port rules to allow traffic on port 3389

7. A point-to-site VPN connection has been established between a workstation named "WorkstationA" and an Azure Virtual Network by a team member. A point-to-site VPN connection between the same Azure Virtual Network and a PC called "WorkstationB" is required. The VPN client package was generated and installed on WorkstationB. You need to ensure that you can create a successful point-to-site VPN connection.
You decide to export the "Workstation A" client certificate and install it on "Workstation B".
Would this solution fulfill the requirement?

A. Yes
B. No

8. As an IT administrator, you must create scripts to add data drives to an existing virtual system. The script is shown below. However, it is not complete.

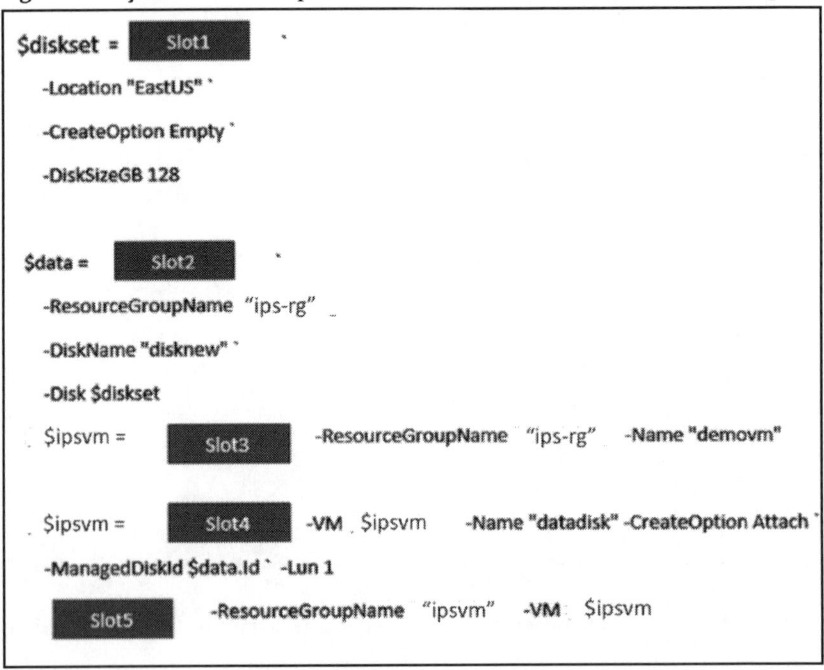

Which of the following would go into Slot4?

A. New-AzDiskConfig
B. New-AzDisk
C. Set-AzDisk
D. Add-AzVMDataDisk

9. A company has an Azure subscription that contains the following resource groups.

Name	Lock Name	Lock type
ips-rg1	None	None
ips-rg2	ipslock1	Delete

The resource group **ips-rg1** contains the following resources.

Name	Type	Lock Name	Lock type
ipsstore2090	Storage account	ipslock2	Delete
ipsnetwork	Virtual network	ipslock3	Read-only
Ipsip	Public IP address	None	None

Would you be able to move the resource **ipsnetwork** from the resource group **ips-rg1** to **ips-rg2?**

A. Yes
B. No

10. A company has two applications, **ipsappA**, and **ipsappB**. Below are the details of each application.

ipsappA - This application is deployed to an Azure Web App. Managed Identity has been enabled for the web app.

ipsappB - This application is deployed to an Azure Container Instance. Managed Identity has been enabled on the container instance.

These programs necessitate the use of a storage account. The usage of secrets must be limited in the solution. Moreover, the duration of ipsappB's access to the storage account should be restricted to 15 days.

To grant ipsappA access to the storage account, which of the following must be used?

A. CORS

B. Shared Access Signatures
C. Access Keys
D. Managed Identity

11. A company is planning to deploy two Azure Kubernetes clusters. Each cluster has different requirements, as given below.

clusterA - You must verify that the nodes in this cluster receive an IP address from the Azure virtual network subnet. Furthermore, the pods are assigned an IP address from a conceptually separate address space.
clusterB - You must guarantee that every pod on the subnet has an IP address and can be accessed directly.
Which of the following must be employed to meet the clusterB requirement?

A. Service endpoint
B. Kubernetes
C. Network Security Groups
D. Azure Container Network Interface

12. A company currently has 2 Azure subscriptions: **ips-staging** and **ips-production**
ips-staging has the following virtual networks.

Name	Address space	Location
vnet-staging-01	10.10.10.0/24	West Europe
vnet-staging-02	172.16.0.0/16	West US

The virtual networks have the following subnets.

Name	Address space	Location
snet-staging-11	10.10.10.0/24	vnet-staging-01
snet-staging-21	172.16.0.0/18	vnet-staging-02
snet-staging-22	172.16.128.0/18	vnet-staging-03

ips-production has the following virtual network.

Name	Address space	Location

vnet-production	10.10.128.0/17	Canada Central

This network contains the following subnets.

Name	Address space
snet-production-01	10.10.130.0/24
snet-production-02	10.10.131.0/24

Can you establish a VNet-to-Vnet VPN connection between **vnet-staging-01** and **vnet-staging-02**?

A. Yes
B. No

13. A company currently has 2 Azure subscriptions: **ips-staging** and **ips-production**
ips-staging has the following virtual networks.

Name	Address space	Location
vnet-staging-01	10.10.10.0/24	West Europe
vnet-staging-02	172.16.0.0/16	West US

The virtual networks have the following subnets.

Name	Address space	Location
snet-staging-11	10.10.10.0/24	vnet-staging-01
snet-staging-21	172.16.0.0/18	vnet-staging-02
snet-staging-22	172.16.128.0/18	vnet-staging-03

ips-production has the following virtual network.

Name	Address space	Location
vnet-production	10.10.128.0/17	Canada Central

This network contains the following subnets.

Name	Address space
snet-production-01	10.10.130.0/24
snet-production-02	10.10.131.0/24

Can you establish a peering connection between **vnet-staging-01** and **vnet-staging-02**?

A. Yes

B. No

14. A company has the following resources defined as part of its Azure subscription.

Name	Type	Location	Resource group
ips-rg1	Resource Group	East US	Not applicable
ips-rg2	Resource Group	West Europe	Not applicable
ips-rg3	Resource Group	North Europe	Not applicable
ips-network1	Virtual network	Central US	ips-rg1
ips-network2	Virtual network	West US	ips-rg2
ipsvm1	Virtual machine	West US	ips-rg3

The simulated machine ipsvm1 is a member of the ips-network2 virtual network. A network interface named ipssecnic is attached to the virtual machine. You must first build an ipssecnic network interface and then attach it to the virtual machine.
You choose the ips-rg2 resource group and the West US region for ipssecnic.
Would this suffice as a solution?

A. Yes

B. No

15. You want to set up a virtual network subnet with five virtual machines.
A public IP address and a private IP address will be assigned to each virtual machine.
Inbound and outbound security policies must be same for each virtual machine.
What is the bare minimum of network interfaces you require?

A. 20

B. 15
C. 10
D. 5

16. You would want to set up an Azure storage account for your firm. The following requirements must be met by the storage account.

- Support for hot, cool, and archive blob levels should be possible.
- It should be able to provide fault tolerance if the Azure region with the storage account is hit by a disaster.
- Costs should be kept to a minimum.

To create the storage account, run the command listed below.

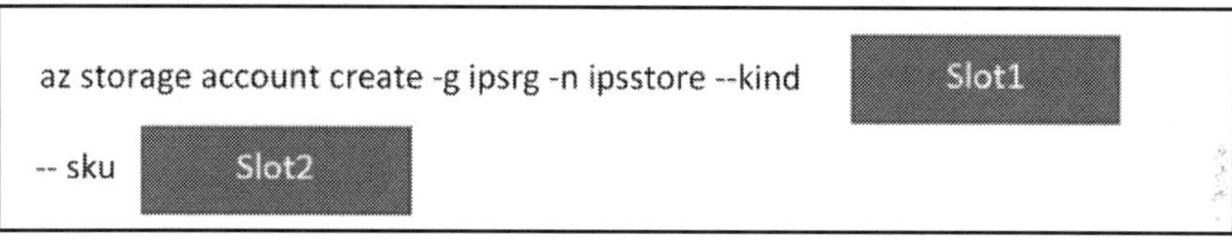

Which of the following would go into Slot2?

A. Standard_LRS
B. Standard_GRS
C. Standard_RAGRS
D. Premium_LRS

17. As an IT admin, you have to develop scripts that need to be used to add data disks to an existing virtual machine. Below is the incomplete script.

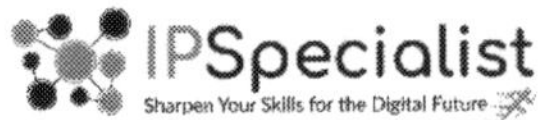

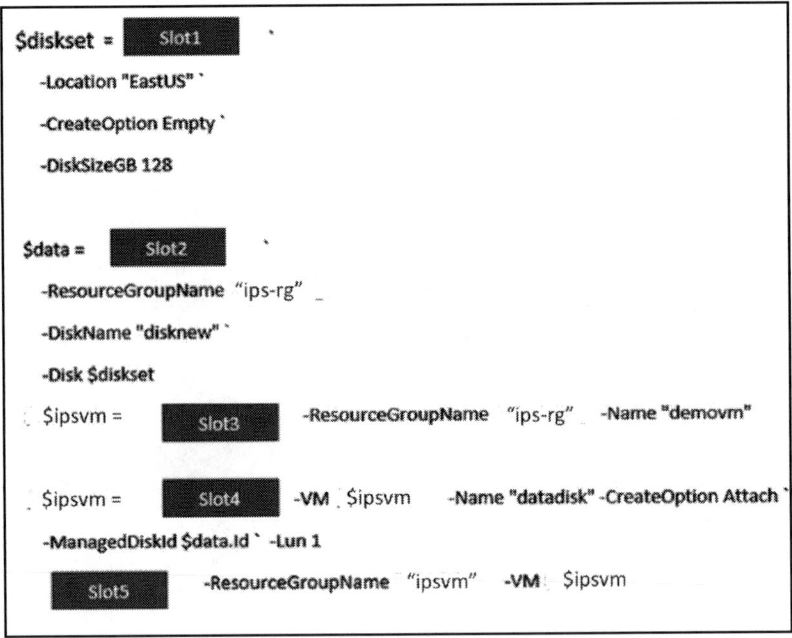

```
$diskset = Slot1 `
  -Location "EastUS" `
  -CreateOption Empty `
  -DiskSizeGB 128

$data = Slot2 `
  -ResourceGroupName "ips-rg" _
  -DiskName "disknew" `
  -Disk $diskset
$ipsvm = Slot3 -ResourceGroupName "ips-rg" -Name "demovm"

$ipsvm = Slot4 -VM $ipsvm -Name "datadisk" -CreateOption Attach `
  -ManagedDiskId $data.Id ` -Lun 1
  Slot5 -ResourceGroupName "ipsvm" -VM $ipsvm
```

Which of the following would go into Slot5?

A. Set-AzVM
B. Get-AzVM
C. Update-AzVM
D. New-AzVM

18. A team member has created a point-to-site VPN connection between a computer named "WorkstationA" and an Azure Virtual Network. Another point-to-site VPN connection needs to be made between the same Azure Virtual Network and a computer named "WorkstationB." On "WorkstationB," a VPN client package was created and installed. You must ensure that a successful point-to-site VPN connection can be established.
You choose to install the "Workstation A" client certificate on Workstation B" after exporting the "Workstation A" client certificate.
Is this the best solution for the job?

A. Yes
B. No

19. You have an ipsstore storage account. Using the file service, you have built a file share called demo. Users must be able to connect to the file sharing from their personal computers. To offer connectivity, which of the following ports should be open?

A. 80
B. 445
C. 3389
D. 443

20. A business has created a storage account as part of their Azure subscription. ipsstore is the name of the storage account. They've also set up a demo file-sharing system. They need to use a UNC path to access the files on the file share.
To ensure that the correct UNC path is provided, fill in the following blocks.

Which of the following needs to go into Slot1?

A. blob.core.windows.net
B. file
C. portal.azure.com
D. ipsstore

21. A business has created a storage account as part of their Azure subscription. The ipsstore is the name of the storage account. They've also set up a demo file-sharing system. They need to use a UNC path to access the files on the file share.
To ensure that the correct UNC path is provided, fill in the following blocks.

Which of the following needs to go into Slot2?

A. blob.core.windows.net
B. file.core.windows.net

C. portal.azure.com
D. ipsstore

22. A business has created a storage account as part of their Azure subscription. An ipsstore is the name of the storage account. They've also set up a demo file-sharing system. They need to use a UNC path to access the files on the file share. To ensure that the correct UNC path is provided, fill in the following blocks.

Which of the following needs to go into Slot3?

A. blob.core.windows.net
B. file.core.windows.net
C. demo
D. ipsstore

23. In Azure, a company has created a Virtual Machine. On the Virtual machine, a web server listening on port 80 and a DNS server has been set up. The virtual machine's network interface has a network security group associated with it. The NSG's rules are listed below.

Inbound Rules

PRIORITY	NAME	PORT	PROTOCOL	SOURCE	DESTINATION
100	⚠ RuleA	50-60	Any	Any	Any
110	⚠ Allow_rdp	3389	Any	Any	Any
120	RuleB	50-500	TCP	Any	Any
65000	AllowVnetInBound	Any	Any	VirtualNetwork	VirtualNetwork
65001	AllowAzureLoadBalancerInBound	Any	Any	AzureLoadBalancer	Any
65500	DenyAllInBound	Any	Any	Any	Any

Outbound Rules

PRIORITY	NAME	PORT	PROTOCOL	SOURCE	DESTINATION
100	RuleC	80	Any	Any	Any
65000	AllowVnetOutBound	Any	Any	VirtualNetwork	VirtualNetwork
65001	AllowInternetOutBound	Any	Any	Any	Internet
65500	DenyAllOutBound	Any	Any	Any	Any

Please select all server(s) that internet users will connect to on the Virtual machine if RuleB is deleted.

A. web server only
B. DNS server only
C. RDP server only
D. RDP, web, and DNS servers

24. Your company has set up a storage account in Azure, as shown below.

Resource group (change) ipspecialist-rg	Performance/Access tier Standard/Hot
Status Primary: Available	Replication Locally-redundant storage (LRS)
Location UK South	Account kind StorageV2 (general purpose v2)
Subscription (change) Pay-As-You-Go	
Subscription ID baaa99b3-1d19-4c5e-90e1-39d55de5fc6e	
Tags (change) Click here to add tags	

The company needs to allow only connections to the storage account from an IP address range of 51.107.2.0 to 51.107.2.255. From which of the following section of the storage account would you modify to fulfill this requirement?

A. Advanced security
B. Firewall and virtual networks
C. Lifecycle Management
D. Soft Delete

25. Your company has set up a storage account in Azure, as shown below.

Resource group (change) ipspecialist-rg	Performance/Access tier Standard/Hot
Status Primary: Available	Replication Locally-redundant storage (LRS)
Location UK South	Account kind StorageV2 (general purpose v2)
Subscription (change) Pay-As-You-Go	
Subscription ID baaa99b3-1d19-4c5e-90e1-39d55de5fc6e	
Tags (change) Click here to add tags	

Any blob data that might be unintentionally deleted must be kept. The erased data must be kept for a period of 14 days. To meet this criterion, which of the following sections of the storage account would you change?

A. Advanced security
B. Firewall and virtual networks
C. Lifecycle Management
D. Soft Delete

26. A corporation wishes to use a Resource Manager template to install a virtual machine. The Azure CLI commands must be used to submit the template. The template is saved in the storage file.json.
You need to complete the below CLI command.

```
az group create --name   ips-rg    --location "Central US"
az  SLOT 1  group create \
  --name    ipsdeployment  \
  --resource-group   ips-rg   \
  SLOT 2  storage.json \
```

Which of the following would go into SLOT 1?

A. deployment
B. template
C. resource
D. vm

27. You need to complete the below CLI command.

```
az group create --name   ips-rg    --location "Central US"
az [SLOT 1] group create \
  --name    ipsdeployment  \
  --resource-group   ips-rg    \
  [SLOT 2] storage.json \
```

Which of the following would go into SLOT 2?

A. --template
B. --template-file
C. --template-uri
D. --template-resource

28. A company has set up an Azure subscription and a tenant. They want to ensure that only Virtual Machines of a particular SKU size can be launched in their Azure account.
The implementation of Role-Based access control is decided.
Does this fulfill the requirement?

A. Yes
B. No

29. A company has set up an Azure subscription and a tenant. They want to ensure that only Virtual Machines of a particular SKU size can be launched in their Azure account.
The implementation of Azure locks is decided.
Does this fulfill the requirement?

A. Yes
B. No

30. A company has set up an Azure subscription and a tenant. They want to ensure that only Virtual Machines of a particular SKU size can be launched in their Azure account.
The implementation of Azure policies is decided.
Does this fulfill the requirement?

A. Yes
B. No

31. A company plans to use Azure Network watcher to perform the following tasks

- Find out if a network security rule prevents a network packet from reaching a virtual machine hosted in an Azure virtual network.
- Find out if there is outbound connectivity between an Azure virtual machine and an external host.

Which of the following Network watcher feature would you use for the following requirement?
"Find out if a network security rule is preventing a network packet from reaching a virtual machine hosted in an Azure virtual network".

A. Next Hop
B. Packet Capture
C. Traffic Analysis
D. IP Flow Verify

32. A company has set up an Azure subscription and a tenant. They want to ensure that only Virtual Machines of a particular SKU size can be launched in their Azure account.
The implementation of Azure locks is decided.
Does this fulfill the requirement?

A. Yes
B. No

33. A company plans to use Azure Network watcher to perform the following tasks

- Find out if a network security rule prevents a network packet from reaching a virtual machine hosted in an Azure virtual network.

- Find out if there is outbound connectivity between an Azure virtual machine and an external host.

Which of the following Network watcher feature would you use for the following requirement?
"Find out if there is outbound connectivity between an Azure virtual machine and an external host."

A. Next Hop
B. Connection Monitor
C. Traffic Analysis
D. IP Flow Verify

34. A company plans to deploy an application to a set of Virtual Machines in an Azure network. The company needs an SLA of 99.99% for the application hosted on the Virtual machines. Which of the following should be implemented to guarantee an SLA of 99.99% on the infrastructure level?

A. Deploy single virtual machines across multiple regions
B. Assign a standard public IP address to the virtual machines
C. Deploy the virtual machines across availability zones
D. Make the virtual machines part of an availability set

35. Your company wants to provision an Azure storage account. The storage account needs to meet the following requirements.

- It should be able to support hot, cool, and archive blob tiers.
- It should be able to provide fault tolerance if a disaster hits the Azure region, which has the storage account.
- Should minimize costs.

You need to complete the below command to create the storage account.

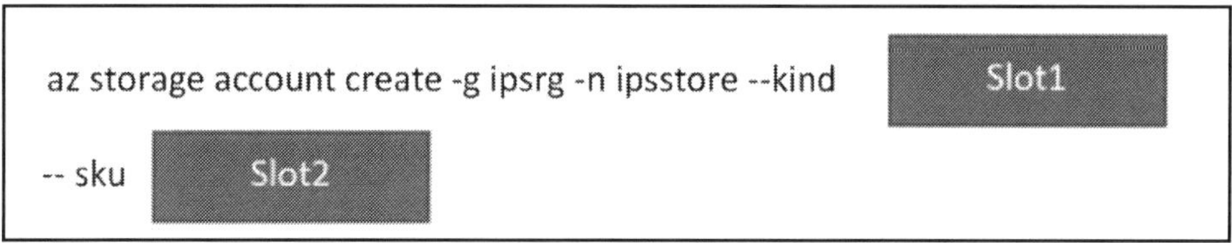

Which of the following would go into Slot1?

A. FileStorage
B. Table
C. BlockBlobStorage
D. StorageV2

36. A team has set up Log Analytics for a virtual machine named **demovm**. They are running the following query in the Log Analytics Workspace.

```
Perf
| where ObjectName =="Processor" and CounterName == "% Processor Time"
| where TimeGenerated between (startofweek(ago(9d)) .. endofweek(ago(2d)))
| summarize avg(CounterValue) by Computer , bin(TimeGenerated, 5min)
| render timechart
```

If a query is run on Monday, then the query will return events from the last.

A. 7 days
B. 11 days
C. 14 days
D. 16 days

37. A team has set up Log Analytics for a virtual machine named **demovm**. They are running the following query in the Log Analytics Workspace.

```
Perf
| where ObjectName =="Processor" and CounterName == "% Processor Time"
| where TimeGenerated between (startofweek(ago(9d)) .. endofweek(ago(2d)))
| summarize avg(CounterValue) by Computer , bin(TimeGenerated, 5min)
| render timechart
```

In which of the below format will the data be displayed?

A. graph that has the Computer values on the Y-axis
B. graph that has the avg(CounterValue) values on the Y-axis
C. table that has 2 columns
D. table that has 3 columns

38. Your company currently has a Site-to-Site connection with an Azure Virtual Private network. The VPN device allocated on the on-premises side will change its public IP address. You have to ensure the Site-to-Site VPN connection continues to work after the change. Which of the following steps would you need to carry out after the change in the public IP address on the on-premises VPN device, ensuring minimum connection downtime? Choose 3 answers from the options given below.

A. Stop the VPN connection.
B. Remove the VPN connection
C. Modify the VPN gateway address
D. Modify the local gateway IP address
E. Recreate the VPN connection

39. A company has an application deployed across a set of virtual machines. Users connect to the application either using point-to-site VPN or site-to-site VPN connections. You need to ensure that connections to the application are spread across all virtual machines. Which of the following could you set up for this requirement? Choose 2 answers from the options given below.

A. An Internal Load Balancer
B. A Public Load Balancer
C. An Azure Application Gateway
D. An Azure Content Delivery Network

40. A company has set up an Azure subscription. They have provisioned a storage account and are currently using the BLOB service. They want to assign permissions to 3 user groups.
GroupA: This group should have access to the storage account management.
GroupB: This group should be able to control storage account containers.
GroupC: Full access to Azure Storage blob containers and data, including POSIX access control, should be granted to this group.
You must assign the relevant Role-Based Access Control, ensuring the privilege of the least access.
Which of the following would you assign to GroupA?

A. Owner
B. Contributor
C. Storage Blob Data Contributor

D. Storage Account Contributor

41. A company has set up an Azure subscription. They have provisioned a storage account and are currently using the BLOB service. They want to assign permissions to 3 user groups.
GroupA: This group should have access to the storage account management.
GroupB: This group should be able to control storage account containers.
GroupC: Full access to Azure Storage blob containers and data, including POSIX access control, should be granted to this group.
You must assign the relevant Role-Based Access Control, ensuring the privilege of the least access.
Which of the following would you assign to GroupB?

A. Owner
B. Contributor
C. Storage Blob Data Contributor
D. Storage Account Contributor

42. A company has set up an Azure subscription. They have provisioned a storage account and are currently using the BLOB service. They want to assign permissions to 3 user groups.
GroupA: This group should have access to the storage account management.
GroupB: This group should be able to control storage account containers.
GroupC: Full access to Azure Storage blob containers and data, including POSIX access control, should be granted to this group.
You must assign the relevant Role-Based Access Control, ensuring the privilege of the least access.
Which of the following would you assign to GroupC?

A. Owner
B. Storage Blob Data Owner
C. Storage Blob Data Contributor
D. Storage Account Contributor

43. A company is planning to use the Azure Import/Export service to move data out of its Azure Storage account. Which of the following service could be used when defining the Azure Export job?

A. File storage
B. Blob storage
C. Queue storage
D. Table storage

44. As an IT admin, you have to develop scripts that need to be used to add data disks to an existing virtual machine. Below is the incomplete script.

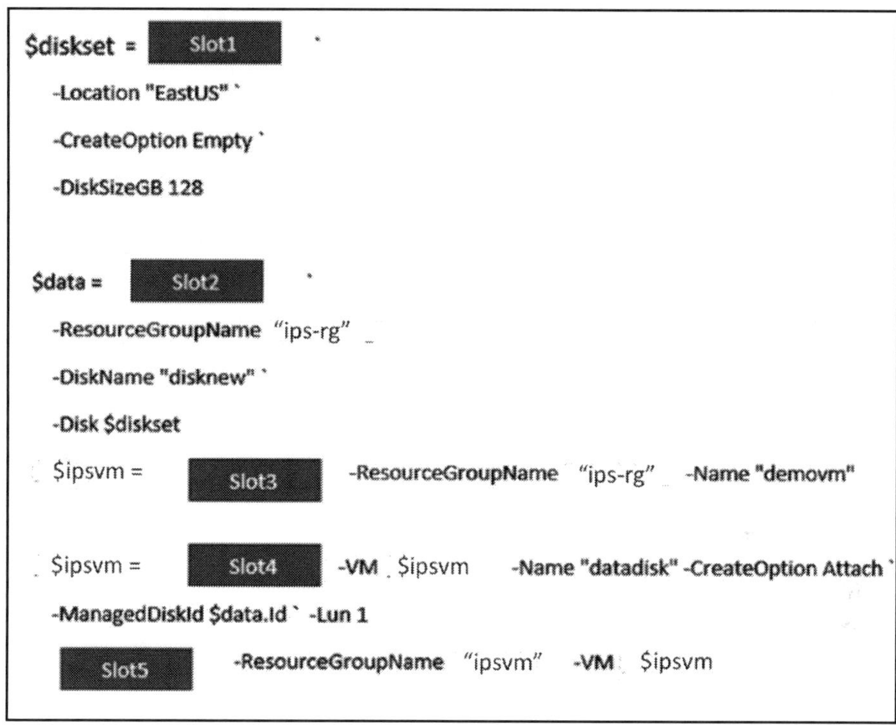

Which of the following would go into Slot1?

A. New-AzDisk
B. Add-AzVMDataDisk
C. New-AzDiskConfig
D. Set-AzDisk

45. As an IT admin, you have to develop scripts that need to be used to add data disks to an existing virtual machine. Below is the incomplete script.

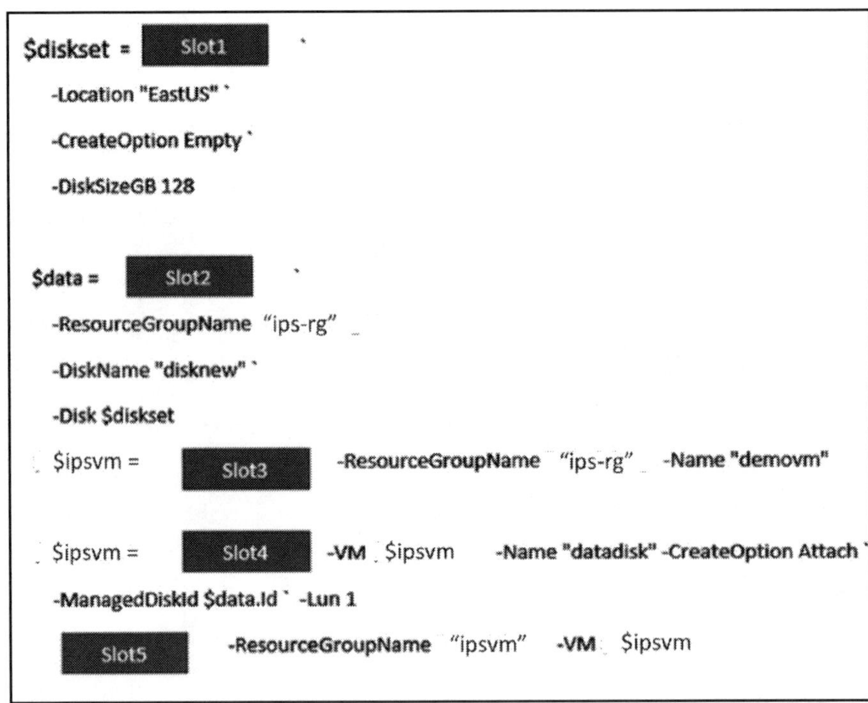

Which of the following would go into Slot2?

A. New-AzDisk
B. Add-AzVMDataDisk
C. New-AzDiskConfig
D. Set-AzDisk

46. As an IT admin, you have to develop scripts that need to be used to add data disks to an existing virtual machine. Below is the incomplete script.

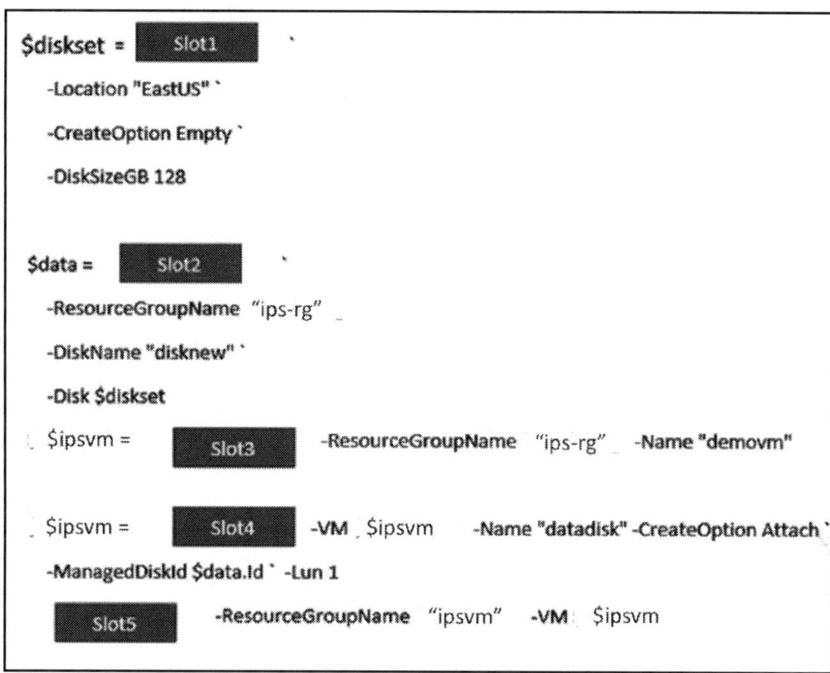

Which of the following would go into Slot3?

A. Update-AzVM
B. Get-AzVM
C. New-AzVM
D. Set-AzVM

47. As an IT admin, you have to develop scripts that need to be used to add data disks to an existing virtual machine. Below is the incomplete script.

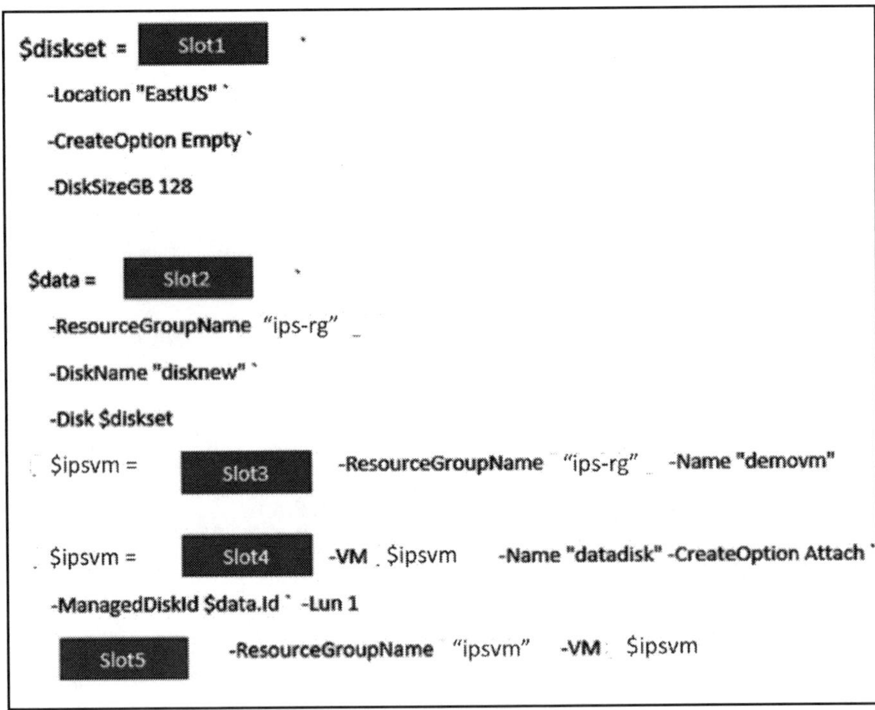

Which of the following would go into Slot4?

A. New-AzDisk
B. New-AzDiskConfig
C. Set-AzDisk
D. Add-AzVMDataDisk

48. You have an Azure virtual machine based on the Windows Server 2016 image. You implement Azure backup for the virtual machine. You want to restore the virtual machine by using the Replace existing option. You need to go ahead and replace the virtual machine using the Azure Backup option. What needs to be done among the following?

A. Create a custom image
B. Allocate a new disk
C. Stop the virtual machine
D. Enable encryption on the disk

49. You have an Azure subscription named **ipsstaging**. Under the subscription, you create a resource group named **ips-rg**
Then you create an Azure policy based on the "Not allowed resources types" definition. Here you define the parameters as Microsoft.Network. Virtual networks the not allowed resource type. You assign this policy to the Tenant Root Group. A Virtual Network does not already exist in this subscription.
Would you be able to create a virtual machine in the **ips-rg** resource group?

A. Yes
B. No

50. A company currently has the following networks defined in Azure.

Name	Address space
ips-vnet1	10.1.0.0/16
ips-vnet2	10.2.0.0/16
ips-vnet3	10.3.0.0/16

All virtual networks host virtual machines with varying workloads. A virtual machine named **ips-detect** is hosted in **ips-vnet2**. This virtual machine will have intrusion detection software installed on it. All traffic on all virtual networks must be routed via this virtual machine.
You need to complete the required steps for implementing this requirement.
You are going to create the virtual network peering connection for all of the virtual networks. Which of the following is important to set for the virtual network peering connection?

A. Set the forwarded traffic settings as Enabled
B. Set the virtual network deployment model as Classic
C. Set the virtual network access settings as Disabled
D. Enable "Allow gateway transit."

51. A company currently has the following networks defined in Azure.

Name	Address space
ips-vnet1	10.1.0.0/16

ips-vnet2	10.2.0.0/16
ips-vnet3	10.3.0.0/16

All virtual networks host virtual machines with varying workloads. A virtual machine named **ips-detect** is hosted in **ips-vnet2**. This virtual machine will have intrusion detection software installed on it. All traffic on all virtual networks must be routed via this virtual machine.

You need to complete the required steps for implementing this requirement.

Which of the following would you need to create additional to ensure that traffic is sent via the virtual machine hosting the intrusion software?

A. Add an address space
B. A new route table
C. Add a service endpoint
D. Add DNS servers

52. A company currently has the following networks defined in Azure.

Name	Address space
ips-vnet1	10.1.0.0/16
ips-vnet2	10.2.0.0/16
ips-vnet3	10.3.0.0/16

All virtual networks host virtual machines with varying workloads. A virtual machine named **ips-detect** is hosted in **ips-vnet2**. This virtual machine will have intrusion detection software installed on it. All traffic on all virtual networks must be routed via this virtual machine.

You need to complete the required steps for implementing this requirement.

Which of the following needs to be enabled on the virtual machine **ips-detect?**

A. Enable the identity for the virtual machine
B. Add an extension to the virtual machine
C. Enable IP forwarding
D. Change the size of the virtual machine

53. A company is planning to use Azure for the various services they offer. They want to ensure that they can bill each department for the resources they consume. The use of Azure policies is decided to separate the bills department-wise.
Would this fulfill the requirement?

A. Yes
B. No

54. A company is planning to use Azure for the various services they offer. They want to ensure that they can bill each department for the resources they consume. The use of Azure resource tags is decided to separate the bills department-wise. Would this fulfill the requirement?

A. Yes
B. No

55. A company is planning to use Azure for the various services they offer. They want to ensure that they can bill each department for the resources they consume. The use of Azure role-based access control is decided to separate the bills department-wise. Would this fulfill the requirement?

A. Yes
B. No

56. A company has the following resources deployed to its Azure subscription.

Name	Type	Resource Group
ips-vnet1	Virtual Network	ips-rg
ips-vnet2	Virtual Network	ips-rg
Ipsvm	Virtual machine	ips-rg

The virtual machine **ipsvm** is currently in a running state.
The company now assigns the below Azure policy.

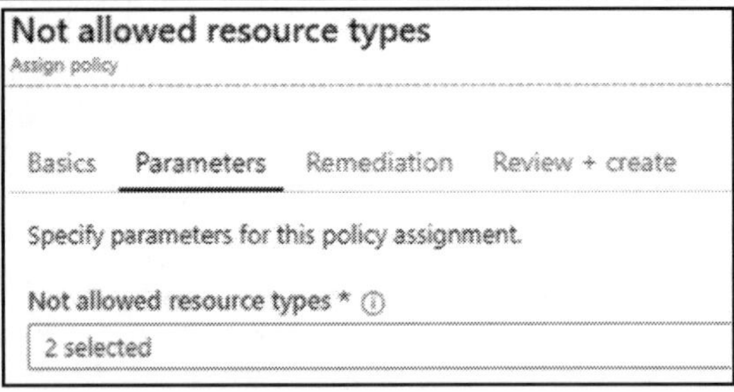

The Not Allowed resources types are

- Microsoft.Network/virtualNetworks
- Microsoft/Compute/virtualMachines

Would an administrator be able to move the virtual machine to another resource group?

A. Yes
B. No

57. A company has the following resources deployed to its Azure subscription.

Name	Type	Resource Group
ips-vnet1	Virtual Network	ips-rg
ips-vnet2	Virtual Network	ips-rg
Ipsvm	Virtual machine	ips-rg

The virtual machine **ipsvm** is currently in a running state.
The company now assigns the Azure policy below.

Not allowed resource types
Assign policy

Basics | Parameters | Remediation | Review + create

Specify parameters for this policy assignment.

Not allowed resource types * ⓘ
2 selected

The Not Allowed resources types are

- Microsoft.Network/virtualNetworks
- Microsoft/Compute/virtualMachines

Would the state of the virtual machine change to deallocated?

A. Yes
B. No

58. A company has the following resources deployed to its Azure subscription.

Name	Type	Resource Group
ips-vnet1	Virtual Network	ips-rg
ips-vnet2	Virtual Network	ips-rg
Ipsvm	Virtual machine	ips-rg

The virtual machine **ipsvm** is currently in a running state.
The company now assigns the below Azure policy.

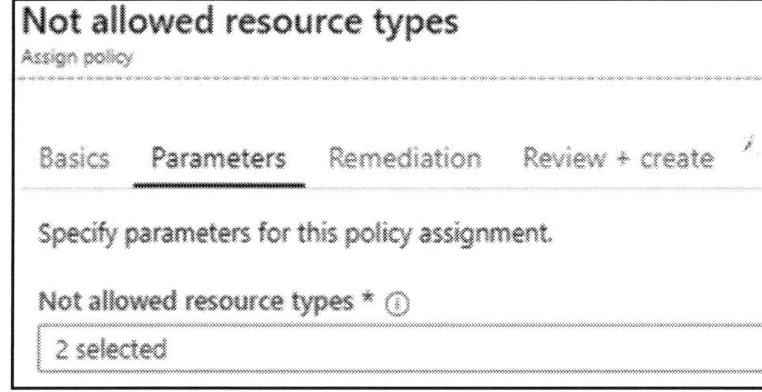

The Not Allowed resources types are

- Microsoft.Network/virtualNetworks
- Microsoft/Compute/virtualMachines

Would an administrator be able to modify the address space of **ips-vnet2?**

A. Yes
B. No

59. A team is currently storing all of its objects in an Azure storage account. They are using the Azure Blob service. They want to create a lifecycle management rule that would do the following.

- Change the objects' tier level to the cool tier if they have not been modified in the past 30 days.
- Archive an object if they have not been modified in the past 90 days.

The Lifecycle rule would be applied to a demo container and a data folder within the demo container. For the Lifecycle rule, you must fill in the JSON sample below.

```
{
 "rules": [
  {
   "name": “ipsrule”,
   "enabled": true,
   "type": "Lifecycle",
   "definition": {
    "filters": {
     "blobTypes": [ "blockBlob" ],
     "prefixMatch": [ " Slot1 " ]
    },
    "actions": {
     "baseBlob": {
      "tierToCool": { "daysAfterModificationGreaterThan": Slot2 },

      "tierToArchive": { "daysAfterModificationGreaterThan": Slot3 }
     },
}
```

Which of the following would go into Slot1?

A. demo
B. data
C. demo/data
D. data/demo

60. A team is currently storing all of its objects in an Azure storage account. They are using the Azure Blob service. They want to create a lifecycle management rule that would do the following.

- Change the objects' tier level to the cool tier if they have not been modified in the past 30 days.
- Archive an object if they have not been modified in the past 90 days.

The Lifecycle rule would be applied to a demo container and a data folder within the demo container. For the Lifecycle rule, you must fill in the JSON sample below.

```
{
 "rules": [
  {
   "name": "ipsrule",
   "enabled": true,
   "type": "Lifecycle",
   "definition": {
    "filters": {
     "blobTypes": [ "blockBlob" ],
     "prefixMatch": [ " Slot1 " ]
    },
    "actions": {
     "baseBlob": {
      "tierToCool": { "daysAfterModificationGreaterThan": Slot2 },

      "tierToArchive": { "daysAfterModificationGreaterThan": Slot3 }
     },
 }
```

Which of the following would go into Slot2?

A. 15
B. 30
C. 90

D. 120

61. A team is currently storing all of its objects in an Azure storage account. They are using the Azure Blob service. They want to create a lifecycle management rule that would do the following.

- Change the objects' tier level to the cool tier if they have not been modified in the past 30 days.
- Archive an object if they have not been modified in the past 90 days.

The Lifecycle rule would be applied to a demo container and a data folder within the demo container. For the Lifecycle rule, you must fill in the JSON sample below.

```
{
 "rules": [
  {
   "name": "ipsrule",
   "enabled": true,
   "type": "Lifecycle",
   "definition": {
    "filters": {
     "blobTypes": [ "blockBlob" ],
     "prefixMatch": [ " Slot1 " ]
    },
    "actions": {
     "baseBlob": {
      "tierToCool": { "daysAfterModificationGreaterThan": Slot2 },

      "tierToArchive": { "daysAfterModificationGreaterThan": Slot3 }
     },
}
```

Which of the following would go into Slot3?

A. 15
B. 30

C. 90
D. 120

62. A team is currently making use of an Azure storage account, as shown below.

Resource group (change)
ipspecialist-rg

Status
Primary: Available

Location
UK South

Subscription (change)
Pay-As-You-Go

Subscription ID
baaa99b3-1d19-4c5e-90e1-39d55de5fc6e

Tags (change)
Click here to add tags

Performance/Access tier
Standard/Hot

Replication
Locally-redundant storage (LRS)

Account kind
StorageV2 (general purpose v2)

A file named **audio.log** has been uploaded to a container called **demo**.
Which of the following is a valid URL that could be used to access the file?

A. https://ipspecialiststore.blob.core.windows.net/audio.log
B. https://ipspecialiststore/demo/audio.log
C. https://ipspecialiststore/audio.log
D. https://ipspecialiststore.blob.core.windows.net/demo/audio.log

63. A team is currently making use of an Azure storage account, as shown below.

Resource group (change)
ipspecialist-rg

Status
Primary: Available

Location
UK South

Subscription (change)
Pay-As-You-Go

Subscription ID
baaa99b3-1d19-4c5e-90e1-39d55de5fc6e

Tags (change)
Click here to add tags

Performance/Access tier
Standard/Hot

Replication
Locally-redundant storage (LRS)

Account kind
StorageV2 (general purpose v2)

A file named **audio.log** has been uploaded to a container called **demo**.
You need to allow users to download the object. The access should be granted for a day only. You need to provide a secure way to access the object. Which of the following would you implement for this purpose?

A. Generate a shared access signature
B. Mark public access on the container
C. Provide access keys
D. Mark public access on the object

64. A company currently has a set of Azure virtual machines. They want to ensure that their IT administrative team gets alert when any of the virtual machines are shut down.
The creation of alerts based on Activity Logs in Azure Monitor is decided.
Would this fulfill the requirement?

A. Yes
B. No

65. A company currently has a set of Azure virtual machines. They want to ensure that their IT administrative team gets alert when any of the virtual machines are shut down.
The creation of alerts in the Azure Advisor service is decided.
Would this fulfill the requirement?

A. Yes
B. No

66. A company currently has a set of Azure virtual machines. They want to ensure that their IT administrative team gets alert when any of the virtual machines are shut down.
The creation of alerts in the Service Health service is decided.
Would this fulfill the requirement?

A. Yes
B. No

67. Case Study.

Overview:
IPSpecialist is an online training provider.
Existing Environment:
The existing environment for IPSpecialist currently consists of the following resources.

- An on-premises data center that hosts an Azure Active Directory forest named ipspecialist.com
- The Active Directory contains users from different departments. IT, Finance, HR

The following table shows the on-premises infrastructure. All servers are running in a virtualized environment.

On-premises server name	Type of Virtualization	Virtual Machine name
ips-ser1	VMware vCenter server	Demovm
ips-ser2	Hyper-V host	demovm-test

Subnet name	Virtual Network name	Address space
SubnetA	ips-net1	10.0.1.0/24
SubnetB	ips-net2	20.0.1.0/24

There are 2 web applications that are hosted on the on-premises environment. The overall details of the web applications are given below.

- Programming Language .Net
- Average memory used for each application – 1 GB

Proposed Environment:

- IPSpecialist is looking towards purchasing an Azure subscription and setting up their environment in Azure.
- Virtual Machines need to have a central location for the storage of files. They would connect to these file shares using SMB.
- All applications and virtual machines need to be migrated onto Azure
- One of the web applications which will be hosted in Azure Web Apps needs to be mapped to a custom domain of ipspecialist-quiz.com in Azure.
- Active Directory users need to be synched onto Azure AD

The following Virtual Networks and subnets are going to be set up in Azure.

Virtual Network name	Address space
ips-net1	10.0.0.0/16
ips-net2	20.0.0.0/16

Technical Requirements:

- The instances for the underlying Web applications should be able to scale up to 5 instances
- Users from the internet should be able to communicate with an Azure VM named "ipspecialistapi" on port 80
- A workflow should be in place for demovm when it is migrated onto Azure. The IT Administrator staff needs to be notified of any changes that occur on this VM
- Minimize costs whenever possible
- There should be an encrypted connection between the on-premises data centers and the VNet "ips-vnet2"
- A custom role needs to be defined known as "ipsrole," which will be based on the reader's role

You need to provision the Azure storage account. You need to complete the below Azure CLI script for this.

```
az storage account create --location "US Central" --name ipsstore \
 --resource-group ips-rg --sku Slot1
```

Which of the following would go into Slot1?

A. Standard_GRS
B. Standard_RAGRS
C. Standard_LRS
D. Standard_ZRS

68. Case Study

Overview:
IPSpecialist is an online training provider.
Existing Environment:

The existing environment for IPSpecialist currently consists of the following resources.

- An on-premises data center that hosts an Azure Active Directory forest named ipspecialist.com
- The Active Directory contains users from different departments. IT, Finance, HR

The following table shows the on-premises infrastructure. All servers are running in a virtualized environment.

On-premises server name	Type of Virtualization	Virtual Machine name
ips-ser1	VMware vCenter server	Demovm
ips-ser2	Hyper-V host	demovm-test

Subnet name	Virtual Network name	Address space
SubnetA	ips-net1	10.0.1.0/24
SubnetB	ips-net2	20.0.1.0/24

There are 2 web applications that are hosted on the on-premises environment. The overall details of the web applications are given below.

- Programming Language .Net
- Average memory used for each application – 1 GB

Proposed Environment:

- IPSpecialist is looking towards purchasing an Azure subscription and setting up their environment in Azure.
- Virtual Machines need to have a central location for the storage of files. They would connect to these file shares using SMB.
- All applications and virtual machines need to be migrated onto Azure
- One of the web applications which will be hosted in Azure Web Apps needs to be mapped to a custom domain of ipspecialist-quiz.com in Azure.
- Active Directory users need to be synched onto Azure AD

The following Virtual Networks and subnets are going to be set up in Azure.

Virtual Network name	Address space
ips-net1	10.0.0.0/16
ips-net2	20.0.0.0/16

Technical Requirements:

- The instances for the underlying Web applications should be able to scale up to 5 instances
- Users from the internet should be able to communicate with an Azure VM named "ipspecialistapi" on port 80
- A workflow should be in place for demovm when it is migrated onto Azure. The IT Administrator staff needs to be notified of any changes that occur on this VM
- Minimize costs whenever possible
- There should be an encrypted connection between the on-premises data centers and the VNet "ips-vnet2"
- A custom role needs to be defined known as "ipsrole," which will be based on the reader's role

You need to configure a VPN connection for **ips-net2**. Which of the following would you need to configure in the virtual network?

A. A gateway subnet
B. An additional address space
C. An express route connection
D. A peering connection

69. Case Study.

Overview:
IPSpecialist is an online training provider.
Existing Environment:
The existing environment for IPSpecialist currently consists of the following resources.

- An on-premises data center that hosts an Azure Active Directory forest named ipspecialist.com
- The Active Directory contains users from different departments. IT, Finance, HR

The following table shows the on-premises infrastructure. All servers are running in a virtualized environment.

On-premises server name	Type of Virtualization	Virtual Machine name
ips-ser1	VMware vCenter server	Demovm
ips-ser2	Hyper-V host	demovm-test

Subnet name	Virtual Network name	Address space
SubnetA	ips-net1	10.0.1.0/24
SubnetB	ips-net2	20.0.1.0/24

There are 2 web applications that are hosted on the on-premises environment. The overall details of the web applications are given below.

- Programming Language .Net
- Average memory used for each application – 1 GB

Proposed Environment:

- IPSpecialist is looking towards purchasing an Azure subscription and setting up their environment in Azure.
- Virtual Machines need to have a central location for the storage of files. They would connect to these file shares using SMB.
- All applications and virtual machines need to be migrated onto Azure
- One of the web applications which will be hosted in Azure Web Apps needs to be mapped to a custom domain of ipspecialist-quiz.com in Azure.
- Active Directory users need to be synched onto Azure AD

The following Virtual Networks and subnets are going to be set up in Azure.

Virtual Network name	Address space
ips-net1	10.0.0.0/16
ips-net2	20.0.0.0/16

Technical Requirements:

- The instances for the underlying Web applications should be able to scale up to 5 instances

- Users from the internet should be able to communicate with an Azure VM named "ipspecialistapi" on port 80
- A workflow should be in place for demovm when it is migrated onto Azure. The IT Administrator staff needs to be notified of any changes that occur on this VM
- Minimize costs whenever possible
- There should be an encrypted connection between the on-premises data centers and the VNet "ips-vnet2"
- A custom role needs to be defined known as "ipsrole," which will be based on the reader's role

You have to ensure that users can communicate with the virtual machine **ipspecialistapi** on port number 80. The creation of an outbound rule in the Network Security Group associated with the virtual machine's network interface is decided.

Would this fulfill the requirement?

A. Yes

B. No

70. A company has an Azure subscription that contains the following resource groups.

Name	Lock Name	Lock type
ips-rg1	None	None
ips-rg2	ipslock1	Delete

The resource group **ips-rg1** contains the following resources.

Name	Type	Lock Name	Lock type
ipsstore2090	Storage account	ipslock2	Delete
Ipsnetwork	Virtual network	ipslock3	Read-only
Ipsip	Public IP address	None	None

Would it be possible to move the resource ipsstore2090 from ips-rg1 to ips-rg?

A. Yes

B. No

71. A company has an Azure subscription that contains the following resource groups.

Name	Lock Name	Lock type
ips-rg1	None	None
ips-rg2	ipslock1	Delete

The resource group **ips-rg1** contains the following resources.

Name	Type	Lock Name	Lock type
ipsstore2090	Storage account	ipslock2	Delete
ipsnetwork	Virtual network	ipslock3	Read-only
Ipsip	Public IP address	None	None

Would it be possible to move the resource ipsip from ips-rg1 to ips-rg2?

A. Yes
B. No

72. A company has an Azure subscription and an Azure tenant named ipspecialist.onmicrosoft.com. The following users are defined in the tenant.

Name	Role	Scope
ipsusr1	Global Administrator	Azure Active Directory
ipsusr2	Global Administrator	Azure Active Directory
ipsusr3	User Administrator	Azure Active Directory
ipsusr4	Owner	Azure Subscription

The user **ipsusr1** creates a new directory named **staging.ipspecialist.onmicrosoft.com**.
New users need to be added to the new tenant.
The company asks **ipsusr1** to create user accounts.
Would this fulfill the requirement?

A. Yes
B. No

73. A company has an Azure subscription and an Azure tenant named ipspecialist.onmicrosoft.com. The following users are defined in the tenant.

Name	Role	Scope
ipsusr1	Global Administrator	Azure Active Directory
ipsusr2	Global Administrator	Azure Active Directory
ipsusr3	User Administrator	Azure Active Directory
ipsusr4	Owner	Azure Subscription

The user **ipsusr1** creates a new directory named **staging.ipspecialist.onmicrosoft.com**.
New users need to be added to the new tenant.
The company asks **ipsusr2** to create user accounts.
Would this fulfill the requirement?

A. Yes
B. No

74. A company has an Azure subscription and an Azure tenant named ipspecialist.onmicrosoft.com. The following users are defined in the tenant.

Name	Role	Scope
ipsusr1	Global Administrator	Azure Active Directory
ipsusr2	Global Administrator	Azure Active Directory
ipsusr3	User Administrator	Azure Active Directory
ipsusr4	Owner	Azure Subscription

The user **ipsusr1** creates a new directory named **staging.ipspecialist.onmicrosoft.com**.
New users need to be added to the new tenant.
The company asks **ipsusr3** to create user accounts.
Would this fulfill the requirement?

A. Yes
B. No

75. A company currently has 2 Azure subscriptions: **ips-staging** and **ips-production**
ips-staging has the following virtual networks.

Name	Address space	Location
vnet-staging-01	10.10.10.0/24	West Europe
vnet-staging-02	172.16.0.0/16	West US

The virtual networks have the following subnets.

Name	Address space	Location
snet-staging-11	10.10.10.0/24	vnet-staging-01
snet-staging-21	172.16.0.0/18	vnet-staging-02
snet-staging-22	172.16.128.0/18	vnet-staging-03

ips-production has the following virtual network.

Name	Address space	Location
vnet-production	10.10.128.0/17	Canada Central

This network contains the following subnets.

Name	Address space
snet-production-01	10.10.130.0/24
snet-production-02	10.10.131.0/24

Can you establish a VNet-to-Vnet VPN connection between **vnet-staging-01** and **vnet staging 02**?

A. Yes
B. No

76. A company currently has 2 Azure subscriptions: **ips-staging** and **ips-production**
ips-staging has the following virtual networks.

Name	Address space	Location
vnet-staging-01	10.10.10.0/24	West Europe
vnet-staging-02	172.16.0.0/16	West US

The virtual networks have the following subnets.

Name	Address space	Location
snet-staging-11	10.10.10.0/24	vnet-staging-01
snet-staging-21	172.16.0.0/18	vnet-staging-02
snet-staging-22	172.16.128.0/18	vnet-staging-03

ips-production has the following virtual network.

Name	Address space	Location
vnet-production	10.10.128.0/17	Canada Central

This network contains the following subnets.

Name	Address space
snet-production-01	10.10.130.0/24
snet-production-02	10.10.131.0/24

Can you establish a peering connection between **vnet-staging-01** and **vnet-production**?

A. Yes
B. No

77. A company has the following virtual machines defined as part of its subscription.

Name	Operating System	Connect to
vmips1	Windows Server 2019	SubnetA
vmips2	Windows Server 2019	SubnetB

- Public IP addresses are assigned to the virtual machines.
- At the operating system level, incoming remote desktop connections have been allowed.
- Both of the subnets are in the same virtual network.
- A network security group named **nsg-ips1** has been assigned to **SubnetA.** This network security group only has the default rules.
- A network security group named **nsg-ips1** has been assigned to the network interface of **vmips2.** This network security group has an additional rule with the following details.
    - Priority: 100
    - Name: nsgrule
    - Port: 3389
    - Protocol: TCP
    - Source: Any
    - Destination: Any
    - Action: Allow

Is it possible to remote desktop into **vmips1** from the Internet?

A. Yes
B. No

78. A company has the following virtual machines defined as part of its subscription.

Name	Operating System	Connect to
vmips1	Windows Server 2019	SubnetA
vmips2	Windows Server 2019	SubnetB

- Public IP addresses are assigned to the virtual machines.
- At the operating system level, incoming remote desktop connections have been allowed.
- Both of the subnets are in the same virtual network.
- A network security group named **nsg-ips1** has been assigned to **SubnetA.** This network security group only has the default rules.
- A network security group named **nsg-ips1** has been assigned to the network interface of **vmips2.** This network security group has an additional rule with the following details.
- Priority: 100

- Name: nsgrule
- Port: 3389
- Protocol: TCP
- Source: Any
- Destination: Any
- Action: Allow

Is it possible to remote desktop into **vmips2** from the Internet?

A. Yes
B. No

79. A company has the following virtual machines defined as part of its subscription.

Name	Operating System	Connect to
vmips1	Windows Server 2019	SubnetA
vmips2	Windows Server 2019	SubnetB

- Public IP addresses are assigned to the virtual machines.
- At the operating system level, incoming remote desktop connections have been allowed.
- Both of the subnets are in the same virtual network.
- A network security group named **nsg-ips1** has been assigned to **SubnetA.** This network security group only has the default rules.
- A network security group named **nsg-ips1** has been assigned to the network interface of **vmips2.** This network security group has an additional rule with the following details.
    - Priority: 100
    - Name: nsgrule
    - Port: 3389
    - Protocol: TCP
    - Source: Any
    - Destination: Any
    - Action: Allow

Is it possible to Public IP of **vmips2** from **vmips1**?

A. Yes
B. No

80. A company has the following resource groups defined as part of its Azure subscription.

Name	Region
rg-ips-01	West Europe
rg-ips-02	North Europe

The following virtual machines are then created in the subscription.

Name	Resource group	Region	Operating system
vmips1	rg-ips-01	West Europe	Windows Server 2016
vmips2	rg-ips-01	North Europe	Windows Server 2016
vmips3	rg-ips-02	West Europe	Windows Server 2016
vmipsA	rg-ips-01	West Europe	Ubuntu Server 18.04
vmipsB	rg-ips-01	North Europe	Ubuntu Server 18.04
vmipsC	rg-ips-02	West Europe	Ubuntu Server 18.04

The following recovery service vault is also defined as part of the subscription.

Name	Region	Resource group
vaultips2090	West Europe	rg-ips-01

The company wants to ensure that as many virtual machines as possible are backed up using the recovery services vault **vaultips2090.**
Which of the following virtual machines can be backed up using the Recovery Services vault?

A. vmips1 only
B. vmips1 and vmips3 only
C. vmips1, vmips3, vmipsA and vmipsC only
D. vmips3 and vmipsC only
E. vmips1, vmips2, vmips3, vmipsA, vmipsB, and vmipsC

81. A company currently has the following resources defined as part of its subscription.

Name	Type	Location
vnet-ips	Virtual Network	East US
ip-ips	Public IP address	West Europe
Routetable	Route table	North Europe

The company wants to create a network interface named **nic-ips**. In which of the following region/regions can you create the new network interface?

A. In East US, only
B. In East US, West Europe, and North Europe
C. In West Europe, only
D. In East US and West Europe, only

82. A company has the following resources defined as part of the Azure subscription.

Name	Type
ipscontainer	Blob container
ipsshare	Azure File share
ipsdb	SQL Database
ipstable	Azure Table

The company is planning to use the Azure Import/Export service. From which resource can you export the data using the service?

A. ipscontainer
B. ipsshare
C. ipsdb
D. ipstable

83. Your company has the following resources defined as part of its Azure subscription.

- 100 Azure virtual machines
- 10 Azure SQL databases
- 50 Azure file shares

You need to create a daily backup of all resources by using Azure Backup. What is the minimum number of backup policies you have to create for this requirement?

A. 1
B. 2
C. 5
D. 100

84. A company has the following resources defined as part of its Azure subscription.

Name	Type	Location	Resource Group
rg-ips-1	Resource group	East US	Not applicable
rg-ips-2	Resource group	West US	Not applicable
Vaultips	Recovery services vault	West Europe	rg-ips-1
storeips2070	Storage account	East US	rg-ips-2
storeips2080	Storage account	West US	rg-ips-1
storeips2090	Storage account	West Europe	rg-ips-2
log-ips-1	Log Analytics workspace	East US	rg-ips-1
log-ips-2	Log Analytics workspace	West US	rg-ips-2
log-ips-3	Log Analytics workspace	West Europe	rg-ips-1

The company is planning to configure the Diagnostic settings for the Recovery Services vault to store the Azure Backup Reports.
Which of the following storage accounts can be used to store the backup reports?

A. storeips2070 only
B. storeips2080 only
C. storeips2090 only
D. storeips2070, storeips2080, and storeips2090

85. A company has the following resources defined as part of its Azure subscription.

Name	Type	Location	Resource Group
rg-ips-1	Resource group	East US	Not applicable

rg-ips-2	Resource group	West US	Not applicable
Vaultips	Recovery services vault	West Europe	rg-ips-1
storeips2070	Storage account	East US	rg-ips-2
storeips2080	Storage account	West US	rg-ips-1
storeips2090	Storage account	West Europe	rg-ips-2
log-ips-1	Log Analytics workspace	East US	rg-ips-1
log-ips-2	Log Analytics workspace	West US	rg-ips-2
log-ips-3	Log Analytics workspace	West Europe	rg-ips-1

The company is planning to configure the Diagnostic settings for the Recovery Services vault to store the Azure Backup Reports.
Which of the following Log Analytics workspace can be used to store the backup reports?

A. log-ips-1 only
B. log-ips-2 only
C. log-ips-3 only
D. log-ips-1, log-ips-2, and log-ips-3

86. A company has the following Azure file shares defined in its Azure subscription.

Name	Storage account	Location
ipsshare1	ipsstorage1	West US
ipsshare2	ipsstorage1	West US

The company also has the following on-premises servers.

Name	Folders
ipsserver1	D:\ips1, E:\ips2
ipsserver2	D:\Data

The company then carries out the following tasks.

- Create a new Storage Sync service named **ipssync**
- Created a new Azure File Sync group named **ipsgroup**
- **ipsshare1** has been added as a cloud endpoint in **ipsgroup**
- The servers **ipsserver1** and **ipsserver2** are registered as servers with the Sync service
- **ipsserver1,** along with the path D:\ips1, is added as a server endpoint in **ipsgroup**

Can you now add **ipsshare2** as the cloud endpoint in **ipsgroup**

A. Yes
B. No

87. A company has the following Azure file shares defined in its Azure subscription.

Name	Storage account	Location
ipsshare1	ipsstorage1	West US
ipsshare2	ipsstorage1	West US

The company also has the following on-premises servers.

Name	Folders
ipsserver1	D:\ips1, E:\ips2
ipsserver2	D:\Data

The company then carries out the following tasks.

- Create a new Storage Sync service named **ipssync**
- Created a new Azure File Sync group named **ipsgroup**
- **ipsshare1** has been added as a cloud endpoint in **ipsgroup**
- The servers **ipsserver1** and **ipsserver2** are registered as servers with the Sync service
- **ipsserver1,** along with the path D:\ips1, is added as a server endpoint in **ipsgroup**

Can you add **ipsshare2** along with the path D:\Data as the server endpoint in **ipsgroup.**

A. Yes
B. No

88. A company has the following Azure file shares defined in its Azure subscription.

Name	Storage account	Location
ipsshare1	ipsstorage1	West US
ipsshare2	ipsstorage1	West US

The company also has the following on-premises servers.

Name	Folders
ipsserver1	D:\ips1, E:\ips2
ipsserver2	D:\Data

The company then carries out the following tasks.

- Create a new Storage Sync service named **ipssync**
- Created a new Azure File Sync group named **ipsgroup**
- **ipsshare1** has been added as a cloud endpoint in **ipsgroup**
- The servers **ipsserver1** and **ipsserver2** are registered as servers with the Sync service
- **ipsserver1,** along with the path D:\ips1, is added as a server endpoint in **ipsgroup**

Can you add **ipsserver1** along with the path E:\ips2 as the server endpoint in **ipsgroup.**

A. Yes
B. No

89. A company has the following users defined as part of their Azure AD tenant. The tenant is also synced with an on-premises Active Directory using Azure AD Connect.

Name	Type	Source
ipsusr1	Member	Azure AD
ipsusr2	Member	Windows Server Active Directory
ipsusr3	Guest	Microsoft account
ipsusr4	Member	Windows Server Active Directory

The users have the following attributes.

Name	Office phone	Mobile phone
ipsusr1	111-222-3333	222-333-4444
ipsusr2	null	null
ipsusr3	333-444-5555	444-555-6666
ipsusr4	555-666-7777	null

You have to ensure Multi-Factor Authentication is enabled for all users.
You make the decision to add a mobile phone number for **ipsusr2** and **ipsusr4.**
Would this fulfill the requirement?

A. Yes
B. No

90. Your company has the following users defined as part of their Azure AD tenant. The tenant is also synced with an on-premises Active Directory using Azure AD Connect.

Name	Type	Source
ipsusr1	Member	Azure AD
ipsusr2	Member	Windows Server Active Directory
ipsusr3	Guest	Microsoft account
ipsusr4	Member	Windows Server Active Directory

The users have the following attributes.

Name	Office phone	Mobile phone
ipsusr1	111-222-3333	222-333-4444

ipsusr2	null	null
ipsusr3	333-444-5555	444-555-6666
ipsusr4	555-666-7777	null

You have to ensure Multi-Factor Authentication is enabled for all users.
You make the decision to add an office phone number for **ipsusr2.**
Would this fulfill the requirement?

A. Yes
B. No

91. Your company has the following users defined as part of their Azure AD tenant. The tenant is also synced with an on-premises Active Directory using Azure AD Connect.

Name	Type	Source
ipsusr1	Member	Azure AD
ipsusr2	Member	Windows Server Active Directory
ipsusr3	Guest	Microsoft account
ipsusr4	Member	Windows Server Active Directory

The users have the following attributes.

Name	Office phone	Mobile phone
ipsusr1	111-222-3333	222-333-4444
ipsusr2	null	null
ipsusr3	333-444-5555	444-555-6666
ipsusr4	555-666-7777	null

You have to ensure Multi-Factor Authentication is enabled for all users.
You make the decision to create a new user account for **ipsusr3** in Azure AD.
Would this fulfill the requirement?

A. Yes
B. No

92. Your company has an Azure storage account named **storeips8080**, which has the following properties.

Location	West US
Performance	Standard
Access Tier	Cool
Account type	General-purpose v2
Replication	Read-access geo-redundant storage
Advanced Thread Protection	Enabled

The company wants to change the replication type of storage account from Read-access geo-redundant storage to Zone redundant storage by requesting Azure support for live migration. Which action needs to be completed first in order to meet this requirement?

A. Ensure to change the Replication technique of the storage account
B. Ensure to change the Account kind of the storage account
C. Ensure to change the Access tier of the storage account
D. Ensure to change the performance of the storage account

93. A company is planning to deploy two Azure Kubernetes clusters. Each cluster has different requirements, as given below.
clusterA - Here, you have to ensure that the nodes get an IP address from the Azure virtual network subnet. And the pods receive an IP address from a logically different address space.
clusterB - Here, you have to ensure that every pod gets an IP address from the subnet and can be accessed directly.
Which of the following needs to be used to fulfill the requirement for **clusterA**?

A. Service endpoint
B. Kubernetes
C. Network Security Groups
D. Azure Container Network Interface

94. A company has the following App Service Plans defined as part of its Azure subscription.

Name	Location	Operating System

ipsplanA	East US	Linux
ipsplanB	East US	Windows
ipsplanC	UK South	Windows

The company is planning on deploying the following Azure Web App Instances.

Name	Location	Runtime stack
ipsapp1	East US	.Net Core 3.1
ipsapp2	East US	ASP.NET V4.7

Which of the following App service plans can you use for **ipsapp1**?

A. ipsplanA only
B. ipsplanB only
C. ipsplanA and ipsplanB only
D. ipsplanB and ipsplanC only
E. ipsplanA, ipsplanB, and ipsplanC

95. A company has the following App Service Plans defined as part of its Azure subscription.

Name	Location	Operating System
ipsplanA	East US	Linux
ipsplanB	East US	Windows
ipsplanC	UK South	Windows

The company is planning on deploying the following Azure Web App Instances.

Name	Location	Runtime stack
ipsapp1	East US	.Net Core 3.1
ipsapp2	East US	ASP.NET V4.7

Which of the following App service plans can you use for **ipsapp2**?

A. ipsplanA only

B. ipsplanB only
C. ipsplanA and ipsplanB only
D. ipsplanB and ipsplanC only
E. ipsplanA, ipsplanB, and ipsplanC

96. A development team has just launched an Azure Kubernetes cluster. They have images placed in an Azure container registry. They want to deploy an application to the cluster using an image from the Azure container registry. Which of the following command could be used to fulfill this requirement?

A. docker build
B. docker run
C. kubectl apply
D. az kubernetes deploy

97. Your company has an Azure subscription that contains a Log Analytics workspace named **log-staging**. You have to get the error events from the table named Event. Which of the following query would you run in the workspace?

A. Get-Event Event | where ($_.EventType -eq "error")
B. search in (Event) "error."
C. select * from Event where EventType=="error"
D. Get-Event Event | where ($_.EventType == "error")

98. A company has an Azure subscription that contains the following resource groups.

Name	Location
ipsgrpA	East US
ipsgrpB	West US

The following resources have been deployed to the subscription.

Name	Resource type	Resource group
ipsnic1	Network Interface	ipsgrpA
ipsip1	Public IP address	ipsgrpA

Ipsnetwork	Virtual Network	ipsgrpA
ipsstore1	Storage account	ipsgrpA

The network interface is attached to a virtual machine located in the **ipsnetwork** virtual network.
Would you be able to move the storage account **ipsstore1** to the resource group **ipsgrpB**?

A. Yes
B. No

99. A company has an Azure subscription that contains the following resource groups.

Name	Location
ipsgrpA	East US
ipsgrpB	West US

The following resources have been deployed to the subscription.

Name	Resource type	Resource group
ipsnic1	Network Interface	ipsgrpA
ipsip1	Public IP address	ipsgrpA
Ipsnetwork	Virtual Network	ipsgrpA
ipsstore1	Storage account	ipsgrpA

The network interface is attached to a virtual machine located in the **ipsnetwork** virtual network.
Would you be able to move the network interface **ipsnic1** to the resource group **ipsgrpB**?

A. Yes
B. No

100. A company has an Azure subscription that contains the following resource groups.

Name	Location
ipsgrpA	East US
ipsgrpB	West US

The following resources have been deployed to the subscription.

Name	Resource type	Resource group
ipsnic1	Network Interface	ipsgrpA
ipsip1	Public IP address	ipsgrpA
Ipsnetwork	Virtual Network	ipsgrpA
ipsstore1	Storage account	ipsgrpA

The network interface is attached to a virtual machine located in the **ipsnetwork** virtual network.
If the public IP address is moved to the **ipsgrpB** resource group, would the location of the resource change?

A. Yes
B. No

101. Your company has an Azure subscription. They are planning to deploy 50 Azure virtual machines that need to be part of an Availability Set. You have to ensure that there are enough virtual machines available if the fabric fails or during service periods.
You need to configure the below template for this requirement.

```
{
    "$schema": "https://schema.management.azure.com/schemas/2015-01-
01/deploymentTemplate.json#",
    "contentVersion": "1.0.0.0",
    "parameters": {
        "whizlabsetName": {
            "type": "string",
            "minLength": 1
        }
    },
    "resources": [
        {
            "name": "[parameters(' ipssetName ')]",
            "type": "Microsoft.Compute/availabilitySets",
            "location": "[resourceGroup().location]",
            "apiVersion": "2015-06-15",
            "dependsOn": [],
            "tags": {
                "displayName": " ipsset  "
            },
            "properties": {
                "platformFaultDomainCount": Slot 1,
                "platformUpdateDomainCount": Slot 2
            }
        }
    ]
}
```

Which of the following would go into Slot 1?

A. 1
B. 2
C. 3
D. 4

102. Your company has an Azure subscription. They are planning to deploy 50 Azure virtual machines that need to be part of an Availability Set. You have to ensure that there are enough virtual machines available if the fabric fails or during service periods.

You need to configure the below template for this requirement.

```
{
    "$schema": "https://schema.management.azure.com/schemas/2015-01-01/deploymentTemplate.json#",
    "contentVersion": "1.0.0.0",
    "parameters": {
        "whizlabsetName": {
            "type": "string",
            "minLength": 1
        }
    },
    "resources": [
        {
            "name": "[parameters(' ipssetName ')]",
            "type": "Microsoft.Compute/availabilitySets",
            "location": "[resourceGroup().location]",
            "apiVersion": "2015-06-15",
            "dependsOn": [],
            "tags": {
                "displayName": " ipsset :"
            },
            "properties": {
                "platformFaultDomainCount": Slot 1,
              "platformUpdateDomainCount": Slot 2
            }
        }
    ]
}
```

Which of the following would go into Slot 2?

A. 3
B. 5
C. 15
D. 20

103. A company has two applications, **ipsappA** and **ipsappB**. Below are the details of each application.

ipsappA - This application is deployed to an Azure Web App. Managed Identity has been enabled for the web app.

ipsappB - This application is deployed to an Azure Container Instance. Managed Identity has been enabled on the container instance.

These applications require access to a storage account. The solution needs to limit the use of secrets. Also, ipsappB should only be able to access the storage account for a maximum of 15 days.
Which of the following needs to be used to allow **ipsappB** to access the storage account?

A. CORS
B. Shared Access Signatures
C. Access Keys
D. Managed Identity

104. Your company needs to deploy an application to three virtual machines. You have to ensure that two virtual machines are always available in the event of a data center failure at any point in time.
You make the decision to deploy the virtual machines as part of an availability set.
Would this fulfill the requirement?

A. Yes
B. No

105. Your company needs to deploy an application to three virtual machines. You have to ensure that two virtual machines are always available in the event of a data center failure at any point in time.
You make the decision to deploy the virtual machines as part of a single availability zone.
Would this fulfill the requirement?

A. Yes
B. No

106. Your company needs to deploy an application to three virtual machines. You have to ensure that two virtual machines are always available in the event of a data center failure at any point in time.
You make the decision to deploy the virtual machines across three availability zones.
Would this fulfill the requirement?

A. Yes
B. No

107. Your team needs to deploy an Azure Resource Manager template. This template would be used to deploy 10 Azure Web Apps. The team wants to ensure that the required resources are present in Azure before deploying the template. The implementation needs to minimize costs as much as possible. Which of the following would the team need to deploy as a pre-requisite?

A. An Azure Application Gateway
B. An Azure Load Balancer
C. 10 App Service Plans
D. A single App Service Plan

108. You have an Azure subscription that contains the following resources.

Name	Type
ipsbalancer1	Load Balancer
ipsvm1	Virtual Machine
ipsvm2	Virtual Machine

The virtual machines run a website that has the following configuration.

Name	Physical path	Alias
Root folder	C:\inetpub\wwwroot\ips	/
Temp	C:\inetpub\wwwroot\Temp	Temp

The Load Balancer is configured to route requests across the virtual machines.
A health probe is configured with the below settings.

- Name - ipsprobe
- Protocol - HTTP
- Port - 80
- Path - /Temp/ipsProbe.htm
- Interval - 5
- Unhealthy threshold - 2

You have to ensure the health probe functions correctly. Which of the following would you implement for this requirement?

A. On both virtual machines, create a file named wlProbe.htm in the C:\inetpub\wwwroot\ips\Temp folder
B. On both virtual machines, create a file named wlProbe.htm in the C:\inetpub\wwwroot\Temp folder
C. Change the port number value on the health probe to 8080
D. Change the unhealthy threshold value on the health probe

109. A company has an Azure subscription named staging. The subscription contains the following resource groups.

Name	Location
ipsgrpA	East US
ipsgrpB	West US

The following policies have been assigned.

Policy Definition Name	Parameter	Assigned to
Not allowed resource types	virtualNetworks	staging subscription
Allowed resource types	virtualNetworks	ipsgrpA

Can you create a virtual network in the resource group **ipsgrpA**?

A. Yes
B. No

110. A company has an Azure subscription named staging. The subscription contains the following resource groups.

Name	Location
ipsgrpA	East US
ipsgrpB	West US

The following policies have been assigned.

Policy Definition Name	Parameter	Assigned to

Not allowed resource types	virtualNetworks	staging subscription
Allowed resource types	virtualNetworks	ipsgrpA

Can you create a virtual network in the resource group **ipsgrpB**?

A. Yes
B. No

111. A company has an Azure subscription named staging. The subscription contains the following resource groups.

Name	Location
ipsgrpA	East US
ipsgrpB	West US

The following policies have been assigned.

Policy Definition Name	Parameter	Assigned to
Not allowed resource types	virtualNetworks	staging subscription
Allowed resource types	virtualNetworks	ipsgrpA

Can you create a virtual machine in the resource group **ipsgrpB** that does not have any other resources?

A. Yes
B. No

112. A company has the following virtual machines defined as part of its Azure subscription.

Name	Number of vCPUs	Location	State
ipsvm1	16	West US	Stopped (Deallocated)
ipsvm2	2	West US	Running

The subscription has a limit of 20 vCPUs for the West US region.

The company now wants to deploy the following virtual machines.

Name	Number of vCPUs	Location
ipsvm3	16	West US
ipsvm4	2	West US

Would the company be able to deploy **ipsvm3?**

A. Yes
B. No

113. A company has the following virtual machines defined as part of its Azure subscription.

Name	Number of vCPUs	Location	State
ipsvm1	16	West US	Stopped (Deallocated)
ipsvm2	2	West US	Running

The subscription has a limit of 20 vCPUs for the West US region.
The company now wants to deploy the following virtual machines.

Name	Number of vCPUs	Location
ipsvm3	16	West US
ipsvm4	2	West US

Would the company be able to deploy **ipsvm4?**

A. Yes
B. No

114. You have an Azure storage account in place. You are planning to enable Azure AD Authentication for the storage account. You want to provide a set of user's specific permissions to access file shares using Azure AD authentication. Below are the requirements for the users.
ipsuserA: Here, the user should be given access to read files shares over SMB

ipsuserB: Here, the user should be given access to read, write, delete, and modify NTFS permissions in Azure Storage file shares over SMB.

To guarantee that the least privileged access is granted, the appropriate permissions must be given.

Which of the following RBAC role should be assigned to **ipsuserA?**

A. Storage File Data SMB Share Writer
B. Storage File Data SMB Share Contributor
C. Storage File Data SMB Share Reader
D. Storage File Data SMB Share Elevated Contributor

115. You have an Azure storage account in place. You are planning to enable Azure AD Authentication for the storage account. You want to provide a set of user's specific permissions to access file shares using Azure AD authentication. Below are the requirements for the users.
ipsuserA: Here, the user should be given access to read files shares over SMB
ipsuserB: Here, the user should be given access to read, write, delete, and modify NTFS permissions in Azure Storage file shares over SMB.
You need to provide the proper permissions to ensure the least privileged access is given.
Which of the following RBAC role should be assigned to **ipsuserB?**

A. Storage File Data SMB Share Writer
B. Storage File Data SMB Share Contributor
C. Storage File Data SMB Share Reader
D. Storage File Data SMB Share Elevated Contributor

116. Case Study.

Overview
Ipspecialist is an online training provider. They have an on-premises data center and an Azure subscription. The subscription is linked to a tenant named ipspecialist.com.
Requirements
They want to deploy the following resources to Azure
- A new Azure virtual network with an address space of 10.0.0.0/16. The virtual network is located in the West US region.
- Two Azure Windows virtual machines to host the web tier of an application named ipsapp.

- Two Azure Windows virtual machines to host the database tier of an application named ipsapp.
- Use an Azure Bastion Host for RDP connectivity to the virtual machines.
- They want to deploy the Azure Firewall service for inspecting the traffic that flows out of the web tier.
- They also want to ensure daily backups are taken for the Azure virtual machines. The daily retention period for the web servers would be one week, and for the database servers, 15 days.

The Azure virtual network contains the following subnets

Name	Address space
Webtier	10.0.0.0/24
Databasetier	10.0.1.0/24

Below are the security requirements

- A user of a particular Azure AD group should be able to join their devices to the Azure AD tenant.
- Users who join their devices should use an additional authentication method during the process of joining devices.
- The database servers should only allow traffic from the web servers.
- The security events log for all virtual machines needs to be sent to a Log Analytics workspace. The overview of the Log Analytics workspace created for this purpose is shown below.

Resource group (change) staginggrp	Workspace Name demolog2090
Status Active	Workspace Id 7949f469-aae7-4712-a3a1-a57fb93081f0
Location East US	Pricing tier Pay-as-you-go
Subscription name (change) Pay-As-You-Go	Management services Operations logs
Subscription ID e5250e15-0516-48f0-889b-dae6c15b6529	Access control mode Use resource or workspace permissions

What is the minimum number of policies required for taking the backup of Windows virtual machines hosting the web servers?

A. 1
B. 2
C. 3
D. 4

117. Case Study

Overview

Ipspecialist is an online training provider. They have an on-premises data center and an Azure subscription. The subscription is linked to a tenant named ipspecialist.com.

Requirements

They want to deploy the following resources to Azure

- A new Azure virtual network with an address space of 10.0.0.0/16. The virtual network is located in the West US region.
- Two Azure Windows virtual machines to host the web tier of an application named ipsapp.
- Two Azure Windows virtual machines to host the database tier of an application named ipsapp.
- Use an Azure Bastion Host for RDP connectivity to the virtual machines.
- They want to deploy the Azure Firewall service for inspecting the traffic that flows out of the web tier.
- They also want to ensure daily backups are taken for the Azure virtual machines. The daily retention period for the web servers would be one week, and for the database servers, 15 days.

The Azure virtual network contains the following subnets

Name	Address space
Webtier	10.0.0.0/24
Databasetier	10.0.1.0/24

Below are the security requirements

- A user of a particular Azure AD group should be able to join their devices to the Azure AD tenant.
- Users who join their devices should use an additional authentication method during the process of joining devices.
- The database servers should only allow traffic from the web servers.
- The security events log for all virtual machines needs to be sent to a Log Analytics workspace. The overview of the Log Analytics workspace created for this purpose is shown below.

Resource group (change)	Workspace Name
staginggrp	demolog2090
Status	Workspace Id
Active	7949f469-aae7-4712-a3a1-a57fb93081f0
Location	Pricing tier
East US	Pay-as-you-go
Subscription name (change)	Management services
Pay-As-You-Go	Operations logs
Subscription ID	Access control mode
e5250e15-0516-48f0-889b-dae6c15b6529	Use resource or workspace permissions

Can you send the security events of the virtual machines to the Log Analytics workspace?

A. Yes
B. No

118. Case Study

Overview

Ipspecialist is an online training provider. They have an on-premises data center and an Azure subscription. The subscription is linked to a tenant named ipspecialist.com.

Requirements

They want to deploy the following resources to Azure

- A new Azure virtual network with an address space of 10.0.0.0/16. The virtual network is located in the West US region.
- Two Azure Windows virtual machines to host the web tier of an application named ipsapp.
- Two Azure Windows virtual machines to host the database tier of an application named ipsapp.
- Use an Azure Bastion Host for RDP connectivity to the virtual machines.
- They want to deploy the Azure Firewall service for inspecting the traffic that flows out of the web tier.
- They also want to ensure daily backups are taken for the Azure virtual machines. The daily retention period for the web servers would be one week, and for the database servers, 15 days.

The Azure virtual network contains the following subnets

Name	Address space
Webtier	10.0.0.0/24

Databasetier	10.0.1.0/24

Below are the security requirements

- A user of a particular Azure AD group should be able to join their devices to the Azure AD tenant.
- Users who join their devices should use an additional authentication method during the process of joining devices.
- The database servers should only allow traffic from the web servers.
- The security events log for all virtual machines needs to be sent to a Log Analytics workspace. The overview of the Log Analytics workspace created for this purpose is shown below.

Resource group (change) staginggrp	Workspace Name demolog2090
Status Active	Workspace Id 7949f469-aae7-4712-a3a1-a57fb93081f0
Location East US	Pricing tier Pay-as-you-go
Subscription name (change) Pay-As-You-Go	Management services Operations logs
Subscription ID e5250e15-0516-48f0-889b-dae6c15b6529	Access control mode Use resource or workspace permissions

You need to allow traffic onto certain FQDNs via the Azure Firewall. Which of the following rules would you create for this requirement?

A. Network collection rules
B. Application collection rules
C. NAT collections rules
D. FQDN collection rules

119. A company has 2 Azure subscriptions named "ips-staging" and "ips-production". The "ips-staging" subscription has the following resource groups:

Name	Region
ips-rg1	West Europe
ips-rg2	West Europe

The company has deployed an Azure Web resource named "ips2050" to the ips-rg1 resource group. The "ips-production" has the following resource groups:

Name	Region
ips-rg3	East Europe
ips-rg4	Central US

Would you be able to move the web application "ips2050" to the resource group "ips-rg3"?

A. Yes
B. No

120. Your company has an Azure AD tenant named ipslabs.com. The following users are defined in the tenant.

Name	Role
ipslabusr1	Cloud device administrator
ipslabusr2	User administrator

The tenant also consists of the following Windows 10 devices.

Name	Join Type
ipslabvm1	Azure AD registered
ipslabvm2	Azure AD joined

The tenant also has the following groups defined.

Name	Join Type	Owner
ipslabgrp1	Assigned	ipslabusr1
ipslabgrp2	Dynamic Device	ipslabusr2

Would the user ipslabusr1 be able to add the device ipslabvm2 to the group ipslabgrp1?

A. Yes
B. No

121. A company has deployed the following Azure Load Balancer resources to their Azure subscription.

Name	SKU
ipslabload1	Basic
ipslabload2	Standard

Requests would be load-balanced over three virtual computers by each load balancer. You want to ensure that ipslabload2 can distribute requests evenly among the three virtual machines.

Which of the following has to be implemented?

A. Ensure the virtual machines are running the same operating system.
B. Ensure the virtual machines are created in the same resource group.
C. Assemble the virtual machines in the same virtual network.
D. Ensure the virtual machines are created in the same availability set or virtual machine scale set.

122. An Azure subscription is owned by a company. They plan to upload approximately 6 TB of data to the subscription. They intend to make use of Azure Import/Export. Which of the following can they use as the import data's destination?

A. Azure Data Lake Storage
B. Azure SQL Database
C. Azure File Sync Storage
D. Azure Blob storage

123. A company has an Azure AD tenant. They have users that are also synced with them on-premises environment. The domain contains the following users.

Name	Role

ipslabadmin1	Security administrator
ipslabadmin2	Billing administrator
ipslabusr	Reports reader

The administrator has enabled self-service password reset (SSPR) for all users.

The administrator has enabled the following SSPR settings.

- Number of methods required to reset - 2
- Methods available to users - Mobile phone and Security questions
- Number of questions to register - 3
- Number of questions to reset - 3

The following security questions are chosen.

- In what city was your first job?
- What was the name of the first school you attended?
- What was your first job?

Would ipslabadmin1 be required to answer the security question "In what city was your first job?" to reset their password?

A. Yes
B. No

124. Your company has an Azure subscription, and an on-premises file server named demo server. You must synchronize files with the demo server and Azure using Azure File Sync Service. You already created a sync group. Which of the following three actions will you perform next?

A. Create an Azure on-premises data gateway.
B. Install the Azure File Sync agent on the demo server.
C. Create a Recovery Services vault.
D. Register demo server.
E. Install the DFS Replication server role on the demo server.
F. Add a server endpoint.

125. You must deploy two Azure virtual machines named VM1 and VM2 based on the Windows server 2016. The deployment must meet the following requirements.

- Provide a Service Level Agreement (SLA) of 99.95 percent availability.
- Use managed disks.

You propose a solution to create a scale set for the requirement.

Would the solution meet the goal?

A. Yes
B. No

126. Your company has an Azure account and an Azure subscription. They have created a Virtual Network named ipslabs-net. The following users have been setup.

User	Role
ipslabs-usr1	Owner
ipslabs-usr2	Security admin
ipslabs-usr3	Network Contributor

Which of the following users would be able to add a subnet to the Virtual Network?

A. ipslabs-usr1 only
B. ipslabs-usr2 only
C. ipslabs-usr3 only
D. ipslabs-usr1 and ips-usr2 only
E. ipslabs-usr1 and ipslabs-usr3 only
F. ipslabs-usr2 and ipslabs-usr3 only
G. ipslabs-usr1, ipslabs-usr2 and ipslabs-usr3

127. A company has created a storage account in its Azure subscriptions. The name of the storage account is ipslabstore. They have also created a file share named demo. They need to access the files in the file share via a UNC path. You need to fill in the following blocks to ensure that the right UNC path is provided.

Slot 1	**Slot 2**	**Slot 3**

Which of the following needs to go into Slot3?

A. blob
B. blob.core.windows.net

C. portal.azure.com
D. file
E. file.core.windows.net
F. ipslabstore
G. demo

128. You have an Azure subscription named ipslabstaging. Under the subscription, you create a resource group named ipslabs-rg. Then you create an Azure policy based on the "Not allowed resources types" definition. Here you define the parameters as Microsoft. Network. Virtual networks the not allowed resource type. You assign this policy to the Tenant Root Group, and A Virtual Network does not already exist in this subscription.
Would you be able to create a virtual machine in the ipslabs-rg resource group?

A. Yes
B. No

129. You have an Azure virtual machine based on the Windows Server 2016 image. You implement Azure backup for the virtual machine. You want to restore the virtual machine by using the Replace existing option. You need to go ahead and replace the virtual machine using the Azure Backup option. Which of the following needs to be done?

A. Create a custom image.
B. Stop the virtual machine.
C. Allocate a new disk.
D. Enable encryption on the disk.

130. A company has the following resources deployed to its Azure subscription.

Name	Type	Resource Group
ipslab-vnet1	Virtual Network	ipslabs-rg
ipslab-vnet2	Virtual Network	ipslabs-rg
ipslabvm	Virtual machine	ipslabs-rg

The virtual machine ipslabvm is currently in a running state. The company now assigns the below azure policy.

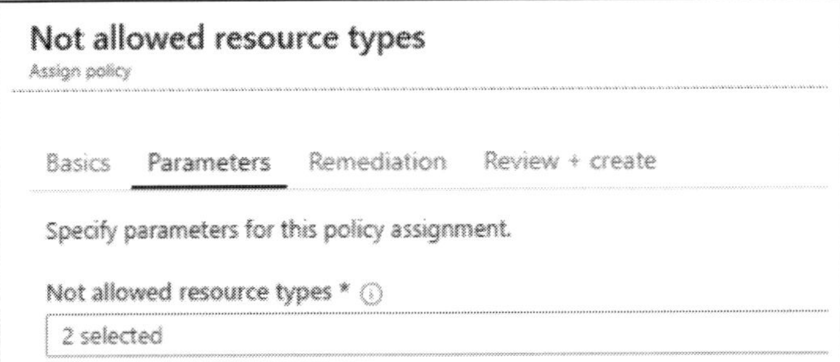

Would the state of the virtual machine change to deallocated?

A. Yes
B. No

131. A company has an Azure subscription that contains the following resource groups.

Name	Lock Name	Lock type
ipslabs-rg1 None	None	None
ipslabs-rg2 Delete	IPSlock1	Delete

The resource group ipslabs-rg1 contains the following resources.

Name	Type	Lock Name	Lock Type
ipslabstore2090	Storage account	IPSlock2	Delete
ipslabnetwork	Virtual network	IPSlock3	Read-only
ipslabip	Public IP Address	None	None

Would you be able to move the resource ipslabstore2090 from the resource group ips-rg1 to ipslabs-rg2?

A. Yes
B. No

132. A company has the following virtual machines defined as part of its subscription.

Name	Operating System	Connect to
vmIPS1	Windows Server 2019	Subnet A
vmIPS2	Windows Server 2019	Subnet B

- Public IP addresses are assigned to the virtual machines.
- At the operating system level, incoming remote desktop connections have been allowed.
- Both of the subnets are in the same virtual network.
- A network security group named ips-lab1 has been assigned to SubnetA. This network security group only has the default rules.
- A network security group named nsg-lab2 has been assigned to the network interface of vmipslab2. This network security group has an additional rule with the following details.
  - Priority: 100
  - Name: nsgrule
  - Port: 3389
  - Protocol: TCP

- Source: Any
- Destination Any
- Action: Allow

Is it possible to remotely connect to vmipslab2's public IP address from vmipslab1?

A. Yes
B. No

133. A company has the following resource groups defined as part of its Azure subscription.

Name	Region
ipslabs-rg1	West Europe
ipslabs-rg2	North Europe

The following virtual machines are then created in the subscription.

Name	Resource group	Region	Operating system
ipslabvm1	ipslabs-rg1	West Europe	Windows Server 2016
ipslabvm2	ipslabs-rg1	North Europe	Windows Server 2016
ipslabvm3	ipslabs-rg2	West Europe	Windows Server 2016
ipslabvmA	ipslabs-rg1	West Europe	Ubuntu Server 18.04
IpslabvmB	ipslabs-rg1	North Europe	Ubuntu Server 18.04
IpslabvmC	ipslabs-rg2	West Europe	Ubuntu Server 18.04

The following recovery service vault is also defined as part of the subscription.

Name	Region	Resource Group

ipslabsvault2090	West Europe	Ripslabs-rg1

The company wants to ensure that as many virtual machines as possible are backed up using the recovery services vault ipslabsvault2090.

Which of the virtual machines listed below can be backed up with the Recovery Services vault?

A. ipslabvm1 only
B. ipslabvm1 and ipslabvm3 only
C. ipslabvm1, ipslabvm3, ipslabvmA and ipslabvmC only
D. ipslabvm3 and ipslabvmC only
E. ipslabvm1, ipslabvm2, ipslabvm3, ipslabvmA, ipslabvmB and ipslabvmC

134. A company has an Azure subscription named ipslabstaging. They also have a resource group named ipslabs-rg. The resource group has created an internal load balancer named “ipslab-internal" and a public load balancer named “ipslab-public”. They want to give a user named “ipslabusr" permission to configure both load balancers. The solution must follow the principle of least privilege.

Which role would you assign the user to allow a health probe to the load balancer “ipslab-public’?

A. Contributor role on ipslab-internal
B. Network Contributor role on ipslab-internal
C. Network Contributor role on ipslabs-rg
D. Owner role on ipslab-internal

135. A company has the following resources.

A file share named ipslabshare in an Azure storage account.

The file share contains a file named ipslab1.txt

An Azure File Sync Service resource.

The following on-premises Windows 2016 servers with their respective file shares and contents.

- ipslabsrv1 D:\ipslabdata1 ipslab.txt, ipslab2.txt
- ipslabsrv2 D:\ipslabdata2 ipslab2.txt. ipslab3.txt
- The following steps are conducted at separate time spans.
    - First, the file share is added to a Sync group named ipslabgroup in the Azure File Sync Service resource.
    - The server ipsrv1 (D:\ipslabdata1) is added as a server endpoint.
    - The server ipsrv2 (D:\ipslabdata2) is added as a server endpoint.

Would ipdlab1.txt from D:\ipslabdata1 share overwrite the file ipslab1.txt on the cloud endpoint?

A. Yes
B. No

136. A company has the following resources defined as part of its Azure subscription.

- ipslabs-rg1 Resource group West US
- ipslabs-rg2 Resource group East Asia
- ipslabstore1 Storage Account West US
- ipslabstore2 Storage Account East Asia
- ipslabvm1 Virtual Machine West US
- ipslabnetwork1 Virtual Network West US
- ipslabnetwork2 Virtual Network East Asia

Currently, the ipslabvm1 virtual machine resides in the ipslabnetwork1 virtual network. You must ensure that the virtual machine resides in the ipslabnetwork2 virtual network. You make the decision to turn off the islabvm1 virtual machine and then add a new network interface to the virtual machine.
Would this fulfill the requirement?

A. Yes
B. No

137. A company is planning to deploy a set of virtual machines across the different system tiers, as mentioned below.

- Web servers Yes 5
- Business Logic No 50
- Microsoft SQL Database Servers No 5

The following requirements need to be met.

- Incoming requests to the Business Logic tier from the web servers must be spread equally across the virtual machines.
- All web servers need to be protected from SQL injection attacks.

Which of the following would you implement for the below requirement?
"All web servers need to be protected from SQL injection attacks."

A. An application gateway that uses the Standard tier

B. An application gateway with WAF
C. A network security group
D. An Internal Load Balancer
E. A Public Load Balancer

138. You have set up a computer named iplabclient1 with a point-to-site VPN connection to an Azure virtual network named ipslabnetwork. A self-signed certificate is used for the point-to-site connection. You must now join another computer named ipslabclient2 to the same virtual network using a point-to-site VPN connection. The VPN client configuration package is downloaded and installed on the ipslabclient2 computer. You make the decision to join the ipslabclient2 computer to Azure AD.
Would this fulfill the requirement?

A. Yes
B. No

139. A company has 2 Azure subscriptions named "ipslab-staging' and "ipslab-production'.
The "ipslab-staging" subscription has the following resource groups

Name	Region	Lock Type
ipslabs-rg1	West Europe	None
ipslabs-rg2	West Europe	Read Only

The company has deployed an Azure Web resource named "ipslabapp2050" to the ipslabs-rg1 resource group.
The "ipslab-production' subscription has the following resource groups.

Name	Region	Lock Type
ipslabs-rg3	East Europe	Delete
ipslabs-rg4	Central US	None

Would you be able to move the web application “ipslabapp2050" to the resource group “ipslabs-rg2"?

A. Yes
B. No

140. A company has 2 Azure subscriptions named “ipslab-staging" and "ipslab-production”.
The “ipslab-staging" subscription has the following resource groups.

Name	Region	Lock Type
ipslabs-rg1	West Europe	None
ipslabs-rg2	West Europe	Read Only

The company has deployed an Azure Web resource named “ipslabapp2050" to the ipslabs-rg1 resource group.
The “ipslab-production" subscription has the following resource groups

Name	Region	Lock Type
ipslabs-rg3	East Europe	Delete
ipslabs-rg4	Central US	None

Would you be able to move the web application “ipslabapp2050" to the resource group “ipslabs-rg3"?

A. Yes
B. No

141. A company has 2 Azure subscriptions named "ipslab-staging" and "ipslab-production”.
The “ipslab-staging" subscription has the following resource groups.

Name	Region	Lock Type
ipslabs-rg1	West Europe	None
ipslabs-rg2	West Europe	Read Only

The company has deployed an Azure Web resource named "ipslabapp2050" to the ipslabs-rg1 resource group.
The "ipslab-production" subscription has the following resource groups

Name	Region	Lock Type
ipslabs-rg3	East Europe	Delete
ipslabs-rg4	Central US	None

Would you be able to move the web application "ipslabapp2050" to the resource group "ipslabs-rg4"?

A. Yes
B. No

142. A company has an Azure subscription named ipslabstaging. They also have a resource group named ipslabs-rg. In the resource group, they have created an internal load balancer named "ipslab-internal" and a public load balancer named "ipslab-public". They want to give a user named "ipslabusr' permission to configure both load balancers. The solution must follow the principle of least privilege.
Which role would you assign to the user to allow the addition of a backend pool to the load balancer *ipslab-internal"?

A. Contributor role on ipslab-internal
B. Network Contributor role on ipslabs-rg
C. Network Contributor role on ipslab-internal
D. Owner role on ipslab-internal

143. A company has an Azure subscription named ipslabstaging. They also have a resource group named ipslabs-rg. In the resource group, they have created an internal load balancer named "ipslab-internal" and a public load balancer named

"ipslab-public". They want to give a user named "ipslabusr' permission to configure both load balancers. The solution must follow the principle of least privilege. Which role would you assign to the user to allow the addition of a health probe to the load balancer "ipslab-public'"?

A. Contributor role on ipslab-internal
B. Network Contributor role on ipslab-internal
C. Owner role on ipslab-internal
D. Network Contributor role on ipslabs-rg

144. Your company has an Azure AD tenant named ipslabs.com
The following users are defined in the tenant.

Name	Role
ipslabusr1	Cloud device administrator
ipslabusr2	User administrator

The tenant also consists of the following Windows 10 devices.

Name	Join type
ipslabvm1	Azure AD registered
ipslabvm2	Azure AD joined

The tenant also has the following groups defined.

Name	Join type	Owner
ipslabgrp1	Assigned	ipslabusr1
ipslabgrp2	Dynamic Device	ipslabusr2

Would the user "ipslabusr1" be able to add the device "ipslabvm2' to the group ipslabgrp1?

A. Yes
B. No

145. Your company has an Azure AD tenant named ipslabs.com
The following users are defined in the tenant.

Name	Role
ipslabusr1	Cloud device administrator
ipslabusr2	User administrator

The tenant also consists of the following Windows 10 devices.

Name	Join type
ipslabvm1	Azure AD registered
ipslabvm2	Azure AD joined

The tenant also has the following groups defined.

Name	Join type	Owner
ipslabgrp1	Assigned	ipslabusr1
ipslabgrp2	Dynamic Device	ipslabusr2

Would the user "ipslabusr2" be able to add the device "ipslabvm1' to the group ipslabgrp1?

A. Yes
B. No

146. Your company has an Azure AD tenant named ipslabs.com
The following users are defined in the tenant.

Name	Role
ipslabusr1	Cloud device administrator

ipslabusr2	User administrator

The tenant also consists of the following Windows 10 devices.

Name	Join type
ipslabvm1	Azure AD registered
ipslabvm2	Azure AD joined

The tenant also has the following groups defined.

Name	Join type	Owner
ipslabgrp1	Assigned	ipslabusr1
ipslabgrp2	Dynamic Device	ipslabusr2

Would the user “ipslabusr2” be able to add the device “ipslabvym1" to the group ipslabgrp2?

A. Yes
B. No

147. A company has deployed the following Azure Load Balancer resources to their Azure subscription.

Name	SKU
ipslabload1	Basic
ipslabload2	Standard

Requests would need to be load-balanced over six virtual computers by the load balancers.

Requests would be load-balanced over three virtual computers by each load balancer.

To ensure that ipslabload1 can load balance requests among the three virtual machines, which of the following must be implemented?

A. Ascertain that the virtual machines use the same operating system.
B. Ascertain that all virtual machines are created in the same virtual network.
C. Assemble the virtual machines in the same resource group.
D. Ascertain that the virtual machines are generated in the same availability set or scale set.

148. A company has deployed the following Azure Load Balancer resources to their Azure subscription

Name	SKU
ipslabload1	Basic
ipslabload2	Standard

Requests would need to be load-balanced over six virtual computers by the load balancers.
Requests would be load-balanced over three virtual computers by each load balancer.
To ensure that ipslabload1 can load balance requests among the three virtual machines, which of the following must be implemented?

A. Ensure the virtual machines are running the same operating system
B. Ensure the virtual machines are created in the same availability set or virtual machine scale set
C. Ensure the virtual machines are created in the same resource group
D. Ensure the virtual machines are created in the same virtual network

149. A company plans to deploy a set of virtual machines across the different system tiers, as mentioned below.

Tier	Accessible from the internet	Number of virtual machines
Web servers	Yes	5
Business Logic	No	50

Microsoft SQL Database servers	No	5

The following requirements need to be met

- Incoming requests to the Business Logic tier from the web servers need to be spread equally across the virtual machines
- All web servers need to be protected from SQL injection attacks

Which of the following would you implement for the below requirement?
"Incoming requests to the Business Logic tier from the web servers must be spread equally across the virtual machines."

A. An application gateway that uses the Standard tier
B. A network security group
C. An application gateway that uses the WAF tier
D. An Internal Load Balancer
E. A Public Load Balancer

150. A company is planning on deploying a set of virtual machines across the different system tiers, as mentioned below

Tier	Accessible from the internet	Number of virtual machines
Web servers	Yes	5
Business Logic	No	50
Microsoft SQL Database servers	No	5

The following requirements need to be met

- Incoming requests to the Business Logic tier from the web servers need to be spread equally across the virtual machines
- All web servers need to be protected from SQL injection attacks

Which of the following would you use to meet the requirements listed below?
"All web servers need to be protected from SQL injection attacks."

A. An application gateway that uses the Standard tier
B. An application gateway that uses the WAF tier
C. An Internal Load Balancer
D. A network security group

E. A Public Load Balancer

151. A company has the following resources defined as part of its Azure subscription.

Name	Type	Location	Resource group
ipslabs- rg1	Resource Group	East US	Not applicable
ipslabs- rg2	Resource Group	West Europe	Not applicable
ipslabs-rg3	Resource Group	North Europe	Not applicable
ipslab-network1	Virtual network	Central US	ipslabs-rg1
ipslabvm1	Virtual machine	West US	ipslabs-rg2

The virtual machine ipslabvm1 is part of a virtual network named ipslab-networkz2. The virtual machine has a network interface named ipslab interface attached to it. You must create and attach a new network interface named the secondary interface to the virtual machine.
You decide to go ahead and create the new network interface in the ipslabs-rg2 resource group and the West US region.
Would this fulfill the requirement?

A. Yes
B. No

152. A company has the following resources defined as part of its Azure subscription.

Name	Type	Location	Resource group
ipslabs- rg1	Resource Group	East US	Not applicable
ipslabs- rg2	Resource Group	West Europe	Not applicable
ipslabs-rg3	Resource Group	North Europe	Not applicable

ipslab-network1	Virtual network	Central US	ipslabs-rg1
ipslabvm1	Virtual machine	West US	ipslabs-rg2

The virtual machine ipslabvm1 is part of a virtual network named ipslab-networkz2. The virtual machine has a network interface named ipslab interface attached to it. You must create and attach a new network interface named the secondary interface to the virtual machine.
You decide to go ahead and create the new network interface in the ipslabs-rg1 resource group and the West US region.
Would this fulfill the requirement?

A. Yes
B. No

153. A company has the following resources defined as part of its Azure subscription.

Name	Type	Location	Resource group
ipslabs- rg1	Resource Group	East US	Not applicable
ipslabs- rg2	Resource Group	West Europe	Not applicable
ipslabs-rg3	Resource Group	North Europe	Not applicable
ipslab-network1	Virtual network	Central US	ipslabs-rg1
ipslabvm1	Virtual machine	West US	ipslabs-rg2

The virtual machine ipslabvm1 is part of a virtual network named ipslab-networkz2. The virtual machine has a network interface named ipslab interface attached to it. You must create and attach a new network interface named the secondary interface to the virtual machine.
You decide to go ahead and create the new network interface in the ipslabs-rg2 resource group and the Central US region.
Would this fulfill the requirement?

A. Yes
B. No

154. A company has the following resources defined as part of its Azure subscription.

Name	Type	Location	Resource group
ipslabs-rg1	Resource Group	West US	Not applicable
ipslabs-rg2	Resource Group	West US	Not applicable
ipslabsvault1	Recovery services vault	Central US	ipslabs-rg1
ipslabvault2	Recovery services vault	West US	ipslabs-rg2
ipslabvm1	Virtual machine	Central US	ipslabs-rg2
ipslabstore1	Storage account	West US	ipslabs-rg1
Ipslabdb	Azure SQL database	East US	ipslabs-rg2

A blob container named "ipslabdata" and a file share named "ipslabfiledata' is created in the storage account.
Which of the following resources can be backed up with the help of the recovery services vault ipslabvault1?

A. ipslabvm1 only
B. ipslabvm1 and ipslabfiledata only
C. ipslabvm1 and ipslabdb only
D. ipslabvm1, ipslabstore1 and ipslabdb.
E. ipslabvm1, ipslabdata, ipslabfiledata and ipslabdb

155. A company has the following resources defined as part of its Azure subscription.

Name	Type	Location	Resource group

ipslabs-rg1	Resource Group	West US	Not applicable
ipslabs-rg2	Resource Group	West US	Not applicable
ipslabsvault1	Recovery services vault	Central US	ipslabs-rg1
ipslabvault2	Recovery services vault	West US	ipslabs-rg2
ipslabvm1	Virtual machine	Central US	ipslabs-rg2
ipslabstore1	Storage account	West US	ipslabs-rg1
ipslabdb	Azure SQL database	East US	ipslabs-rg2

A blob container named "ipslabdata" and a file share named "ipslabfiledata' is created in the storage account.
Which of the following resources can be backed up with the help of the recovery services vault ipslabvault1?

A. ipslabstore1 only
B. ipslabfiledata only
C. ipslabvm1 and ipslabfiledata only
D. ipslabdata and ipslabfiledata only
E. ipslabstore1 and ipslabdb only

156. A company has an Azure AD directory that contains the following users.

Name	Role
ipslabusr1	None
ipslabusr2	Global administrator
ipslabusr3	Cloud device administrator
ipslabusr4	Intune administrator

The Azure AD Tenant has the following device settings
Users can join devices to Azure AD
Additional local administrators on Azure AD joined devices are set to None
The user ipslabusr1 joins a Windows 10 computer to the Azure AD tenant.

You need to identify those users that would be added to the local Administrators group on the computer.

A. ipslabusr1 only
B. ipslabusr2 only
C. ipslabusr1, ipslabusr2, and ipslabusr3 only
D. ipslabusr1 and ipslabusr2 only
E. ipslabusr1, ipslabusr2, ipslabusr3 and ipslabusr4

157. A company has the following resources

- A file share named ipslabshare in an Azure storage account.
- The file share contains a file named ipslab1.txt
- An Azure File Sync Service resource

The following on-premises Windows 2016 servers with their respective file shares and contents.

Name	Share	Contents
ipslabsrv1	D:\ipslabdata1	ipslab1.txt, ipslab2.txt
ipslabsrv2	D:\ipslabdata2	ipslab2.txt, ipslab3.txt

The following steps are conducted at separate time spans
First, the file share is added to a Sync group named ipslabgroup in the Azure File Sync Service resource
The server ipslabsrvi (D:\ipslabdata1) is added as a server endpoint
The server ipslabsrv2 (D:\ipslabdata2) is added as a server endpoint
Would ipslab1.txt from D:\ ipslabdata1 share overwrite the file ipslab1.txt on the cloud endpoint?

A. Yes
B. No

158. A company has the following resources

- A file share named ipslabshare in an Azure storage account.
- The file share contains a file named ipslab1.txt

- An Azure File Sync Service resource

The following on-premises Windows 2016 servers with their respective file shares and contents.

Name	Share	Contents
ipslabsrv1	D:\ipslabdata1	ipslab1.txt, ipslab2.txt
ipslabsrv2	D:\ipslabdata2	ipslab2.txt, ipslab3.txt

The following steps are conducted at separate time spans

- First, the file share is added to a Sync group named ipslabgroup in the Azure File Sync Service resource
- The server ipslabsrv1 (D:\ipslabdata1) is added as a server endpoint
- The server ipslabsrv2 (D:\ipslabdataz2) is added as a server endpoint

Would the file ipslab1.txt overwrite the file ipslab1.txt on the server ipslabsrv1 from the cloud endpoint?

A. Yes
B. No

159. A company has the following resources

- A file share named ipslabshare in an Azure storage account.
- The file share contains a file named ipslab1.txt
- An Azure File Sync Service resource

The following on-premises Windows 2016 servers with their respective file shares and contents.

Name	Share	Contents
ipslabsrv1	D:\ipslabdata1	ipslab1.txt, ipslab2.txt
ipslabsrv2	D:\ipslabdata2	ipslab2.txt, ipslab3.txt

The following steps are conducted at separate time spans.

- First, the file share is added to a Sync group named ipslabgroup in the Azure File Sync Service resource
- The server ipslabsrv1 (D:\ipslabdata1) is added as a server endpoint
- The server ipslabsrv2 (D'\ipslabdata2) is added as a server endpoint

Would the file ipslab1.txt on the server ipslabsrv1 be replicated to the D:\ ipslabdata2 on the server ipslabsrv2?

A. Yes
B. No

160. A company has an Azure subscription. They want to transfer around 6 TB of data to the subscription. They plan to use the Azure Import/Export service. Which of the following can they use as the destination for the imported data?

A. Azure Data Lake Storage
B. Azure File Sync Storage
C. Azure SQL Database
D. Azure Blob storage

161. A company has an Azure AD tenant. They have users that are also synced from their on-premises environment. The domain contains the following users.

Name	Role
ipslabadmin1	Security administrator
ipslabadmin2	Billing administrator
Ipslabadusr	Reports reader

The administrator has enabled self-service password reset for all users.
The administrator has enabled the following SSPR settings

- Number of methods required to reset - 2
- Methods available to users - Mobile phone and Security questions
- Number of questions to register - 3
- Number of questions to reset - 3

The following security questions are chosen

- In what city was your first job?
- What was the name of the first school you attended?

- What was your first job?

Would ipslabadmin1 be required to answer the security question "In what city was your first job?" to reset their password?

A. Yes
B. No

162. A company has an Azure AD tenant. They have users that are also synced from their on-premises environment. The domain contains the following users.

Name	Role
ipslabadmin1	Security administrator
ipslabadmin2	Billing administrator
Ipslabadusr	Reports reader

The administrator has enabled self-service password reset for all users.
The administrator has enabled the following SSPR settings.

- Number of methods required to reset - 2
- Methods available to users - Mobile phone and Security questions
- Number of questions to register - 3
- Number of questions to reset - 3

The following security questions are chosen

- In what city was your first job?
- What was the name of the first school you attended?
- What was your first job?

Would ipslabadmin2 be required to answer the security question "What was the name of the first school you attended?" to reset their password?

A. Yes
B. No

163. A company has an Azure AD tenant. They have users that are also synced from their on-premises environments. The domain contains the following users.

Name	Role
ipslabadmin1	Security administrator
ipslabadmin2	Billing administrator
Ipslabadusr	Reports reader

The administrator has enabled self-service password reset for all users.
The administrator has enabled the following SSPR settings

- Number of methods required to reset - 2
- Methods available to users - Mobile phone and Security questions
- Number of questions to register - 3
- Number of questions to reset - 3

The following security questions are chosen

- In what city was your first job?
- What was the name of the first school you attended?

Would ipslabusr be required to answer the security question "In what city was your first job?" to reset their password?

A. Yes
B. No

164. A company has an Azure subscription and an Azure tenant. The administrator has enabled multi-factor authentication for all users. The administrator needs to ensure that users can lock out their accounts if they receive an unsolicited MFA request from Azure. Which of the following needs to be configured for this requirement?

A. Configure Block/unblock users
B. Configure Providers
C. Configure Notifications
D. Configure Fraud alerts

165. A company has the following resources defined as part of its Azure subscription.

Name	Type	Region

ipslabs-rg1	Resource group	West US
ipslabs-rg2	Resource group	East Asia
ipslabstore1	Storage Account	West US
ipslabstore2	Storage Account	East Asia
ipslabvm1	Virtual Machine	West US
ipslabnetwork1	Virtual Network	West US
ipslabnetwork2	Virtual Network	East Asia

Currently, the ipslabvm1 virtual machine resides in the ipslabnetwork1 virtual network.
You must ensure that the virtual machine resides in the ipslabnetwork2 virtual network.
You create a new network interface and then add the network interface to the ipslabvm1 virtual machine.
Would this fulfill the requirement?

A. Yes
B. No

166. A company has the following resources defined as part of its Azure subscription.

Name	Type	Region
ipslabs-rg1	Resource group	West US
ipslabs-rg2	Resource group	East Asia
ipslabstore1	Storage Account	West US
ipslabstore2	Storage Account	East Asia
ipslabvm1	Virtual Machine	West US
ipslabnetwork1	Virtual Network	West US
ipslabnetwork2	Virtual Network	East Asia

Currently, the ipslabvm1 virtual machine resides in the ipslabnetwork1 virtual network.
You must ensure that ipslabvm1 virtual machine resides in the ipslabnetwork2 virtual network.
You make the decision to delete the ipslabvm1 virtual machine and then recreate the virtual machine in ipslabnetwork2. You also create a new network interface for the virtual machine.
Would this fulfill the requirement?

A. Yes
B. No

167. A company has the following resources defined as part of its Azure subscription.

Name	Type	Region
ipslabs-rg1	Resource group	West US
ipslabs-rg2	Resource group	East Asia
ipslabstore1	Storage Account	West US
ipslabstore2	Storage Account	East Asia
ipslabym1	Virtual Machine	West US
ipslabnetwork1	Virtual Network	West US
ipslabnetwork2	Virtual Network	East Asia

Currently, the ipslabvm1 virtual machine resides in the ipslabnetwork1 virtual network.
You must ensure that ipslabvm1 virtual machine resides in the ipslabnetwork2 virtual network.
You make the decision to turn off the ipslabym1 virtual machine and then add a new network interface to the virtual machine.
Would this fulfill the requirement?

A. Yes
B. No

168. Your company has the following resources deployed to Azure.

Name	IP address	Connected to
ipslabvm1	10.1.0.4	ipslabnetwork1/Subnet1
ipslabvm2	10.1.10.4	ipslabnetwork1/Subnet2
ipslabvm3	172.16.0.4	ipslabnetwork2/Subnet
ipslabvm4	10.2.08	ipslabnetwork3/SubnetB

You then install DNS services on the virtual machine ipslabvm1. The DNS server settings are configured for each virtual network, as shown below.

- DNS servers
- Default (Azure-provided)
- Custom
- 10.1.0.4
- Add DNS server

You must ensure all virtual machines can resolve DNS names by using the DNS service on the virtual machine ipslabvm1. Which of the following would you implement for this requirement?

A. Add service endpoints for the virtual network ipslabnetwork2 and ipslabnetwork3
B. Configure a conditional forwarder for the ipslabym1 virtual machine
C. Add service endpoint for the virtual network ipslabnetwork1
D. Configure virtual network peering connections between all virtual networks.

169. Your company has the following resources defined in Azure.

Name	Type	Resource group	Location
ipslabvaultzogo	Recovery services vault	ipslabs-rg	East US
ipslabvm1	Virtual Machine	ipslabs-rg	East US
ipslabvm2	Virtual Machine	ipslabs-rg	West US

All of the virtual machines run Windows Server 2016.
On the virtual machine ipslabvm1, you back up a folder named ipslabdata as per the following schedule.
After the backup is in place, you want to restore the backup to the virtual machine ipslabvm2.
Which of the following must you implement for this requirement?

A. On the virtual machine ipslabvm1, install the Windows Server Backup feature
B. On the virtual machine ipslabvm1, install the Microsoft Azure Recovery Services Agent
C. On the virtual machine ipslabvm2, install the Windows Server Backup feature
D. On the virtual machine ipslabvm2, install the Microsoft Azure Recovery Services Agent

170. Your company has an Azure virtual machine that runs Windows Server 2016. You must create an alert in Azure whenever two error events are logged to the System log on the virtual machine within an hour. You decide to create a Log Analytics workspace and configure the data settings. You then set up the virtual machine as a data source. You then create an alert in Azure Monitor and specify the Log Analytics as the source.
Would this fulfill the requirement?

A. Yes
B. No

171. Your company has an Azure virtual machine that runs Windows Server 2016. You must create an alert in Azure whenever two error events are logged to the System log on the virtual machine within an hour. You decide to create an Event subscription on the virtual machine. You then create an alert in Azure Monitor and ensure to specify the virtual machine as the source.
Would this fulfill the requirement?

A. Yes
B. No

172. Your organization has a Windows Server 2016 virtual machine in Azure.
When two error events are logged to the System log on the virtual machine within an hour, you must issue an alert in Azure.

On the virtual machine, you decide whether or not to produce Notifications. Then, in Azure Monitor, create an alert and make sure to mention the virtual machine as the source.
Would this fulfill the requirement?

A. Yes
B. No

173. You have to configure Application Insights for a set of applications. Each application has different requirements. Below are the requirements for each application

- ipslabapp1 - Be able to see if users are progressing through the entire business process for the application
- ipslabapp2 - Here, one should be able to analyze the load times and other properties that could influence conversion rates for the application
- ipslabapp3 - Here, one should be able to analyze how many users return to the application
- ipslabapp4 - Here, one should be able to see the places where users repeat the same action over and over again

Which of the following feature of Application Insights could be used for the application ipslabapp1?

A. Impact
B. User Flows
C. Retention
D. Funnels

174. You have to configure Application Insights for a set of applications. Each application has different requirements. Below are the requirements for each application

- ipslabapp1 - Be able to see if users are progressing through the entire business process for the application
- ipslabapp2 - Here, one should be able to analyze the load times and other properties that could influence conversion rates for the application
- ipslabapp3 - Here, one should be able to analyze how many users return to the application
- ipslabapp4 - Here, one should be able to see the places where users repeat the same action over and over again

Which of the following feature of Application Insights could be used for the application ipslabapp2?

A. Impact
B. Retention
C. User Flows
D. Funnels

175. You have to configure Application Insights for a set of applications. Each application has different requirements. Below are the requirements for each application

- ipslabapp1 - Be able to see if users are progressing through the entire business process for the application
- ipslabapp2 - Here, one should be able to analyze the load times and other properties that could influence conversion rates for the application
- ipslabapp3 - Here, one should be able to analyze how many users return to the application
- ipslabapp4 - Here, one should be able to see the places where users repeat the same action over and over again

Which of the following feature of Application Insights could be used for the application ipslabapp3?

A. Impact
B. Retention
C. Funnels
D. User Flows

176. You have to configure Application Insights for a set of applications. Each application has different requirements. Below are the requirements for each application

- ipslabapp1 - Be able to see if users are progressing through the entire business process for the application
- ipslabapp2 - Here, one should be able to analyze the load times and other properties that could influence conversion rates for the application
- ipslabapp3 - Here, one should be able to analyze how many users return to the application
- ipslabapp4 - Here, one should be able to see the places where users repeat the same action over and over again

Which of the following feature of Application Insights could be used for the application ipslabapp4?

A. Impact
B. User Flows
C. Retention
D. Funnels

177. You have set up a computer named ipslabclient1 that has a point-to-site VPN connection to an Azure virtual network named ipslabnetwork. A self-signed certificate is used for the point-to-site connection. You must now join another computer named ipslabclient2 to the same virtual network using a point-to-site VPN connection. The VPN client configuration package is downloaded and installed on the ipslabclient2 computer. You have to ensure that you can establish a point-to-site VPN connection from the ipslabclient2 computer. You decide to set the Startup type for the IPSec Policy Agent service to Automatic on the ipslabclient2 computer. Would this fulfill the requirement?

A. Yes
B. No

178. You have set up a computer named ipslabclient1 that has a point-to-site VPN connection to an Azure virtual network named ipslabnetwork. The point-to-site connection makes use of a self-signed certificate. You now have to establish a point-to-site VPN connection to the same virtual network from another computer named ipslabclient2. The VPN client configuration package is downloaded and installed on the ipslabclient2 computer.
You have to ensure that you can establish a point-to-site VPN connection from the ipslabclient2 computer.
You decide to modify the Azure AD authentication policies.
Would this fulfill the requirement?

A. Yes
B. No

179. You have set up a computer named ipslabclient1 that has a point-to-site VPN connection to an Azure virtual network named ipslabnetwork. A self-signed certificate is used for the point-to-site connection. You must now join another computer named ipslabclient2 to the same virtual network using a point-to-site

VPN connection. The VPN client configuration package is downloaded and installed on the ipslabclient2 computer. You decide to export the client certificate from ipsclient1 and then install the certificate on ipslabclient2.
Would this fulfill the requirement?

A. Yes
B. No

180. You have set up a computer named ipslabclient1 that has a point-to-site VPN connection to an Azure virtual network named ipslabnetwork. A self-signed certificate is used for the point-to-site connection. You must now join another computer named ipslabclient2 to the same virtual network using a point-to-site VPN connection. The VPN client configuration package is downloaded and installed on the ipslabclient2 computer. You decide to join the ipslabclient2 computer to Azure AD
Would this fulfill the requirement?

A. Yes
B. No

181. You have to create an Azure Command-Line Interface script that would carry out the following tasks

- Create a new Azure virtual network with an address space of 10.2.0.0/16
- The virtual network needs to have a subnet with an address space of 10.2.0.0/24
- Create a new private DNS zone named ipslab local
- Create a virtual network link for the virtual network with the DNS Zone

For these criteria, you must finish the CLI script below.

```
Slot 1 create \
--name ipslab-network \
--resource-group ipslabs-rg \
--location eastus \
--address-prefix 10.2.0.0/16 \
--subnet-name SubnetA \
--subnet-prefixes 10.2.0.0/24
Slot 2 create -g ipslabs-rg \
```

```
-n ipslab.local
Slot 3 vnet create -g ipslabs-rg -n virtuallink \
-2 ipslab.local -v ipslab-network -e true
```

Which of the following should go into Slot 1?

A. az network private-dns zone
B. az network vnet
C. az network private-dns link vnet
D. azdns-zone link

182. You have to create an Azure Command-Line Interface script that would carry out the following tasks

- Create a new Azure virtual network with an address space of 10.2.0.0/16
- The virtual network needs to have a subnet with an address space of 10.2.0.0/24
- Create a new private DNS zone named ipslab local
- Create a virtual network link for the virtual network with the DNS Zone

For these criteria, you must finish the CLI script below.

```
Slot 1 create \
--name ipslab-network \
--resource-group ipslabs-rg \
--location eastus \
--address-prefix 10.2.0.0/16 \
--subnet-name SubnetA \
--subnet-prefixes 10.2.0.0/24
Slot 2 create -g ipslabs-rg \
-n ipslab.local
Slot 3 vnet create -g ipslabs-rg -n virtuallink \
-2 ipslab.local -v ipslab-network -e true
```

Which of the following should go into Slot 2?

A. az network private-dns zone
B. az network vnet create
C. azdns-zone link

D. az network private-dns link vnet

183. You have to create an Azure Command-Line Interface script that would carry out the following tasks

- Create a new Azure virtual network with an address space of 10.2.0.0/16
- The virtual network needs to have a subnet with an address space of 10.2.0.0/24
- Create a new private DNS zone named ipslab local
- Create a virtual network link for the virtual network with the DNS Zone

You have to complete the below CLI script for these requirements.

```
Slot 1 create \
--name ipslab-network \
--resource-group ipslabs-rg \
--location eastus \
--address-prefix 10.2.0.0/16 \
--subnet-name SubnetA \
--subnet-prefixes 10.2.0.0/24
Slot 2 create -g ipslabs-rg \
-n ipslab.local
Slot 3 vnet create -g ipslabs-rg -n virtuallink \
-2 ipslab.local -v ipslab-network -e true
```

Which of the following should go into Slot 3?

A. az network private-dns zone
B. azdns-zone link
C. az network vnet create
D. az network private-dns link

184. You have to deploy a web application for your company by using the Azure Web App Service. The backup and restore options should be available for the web application. Costs should also be minimized for hosting the application.
Which of the following would you choose as the underlying App Service Plan?

A. Basic

B. Shared
C. Standard
D. Premium

185. Your company has an Azure subscription that has the following providers registered

- Authorization
- Automation
- Resources
- Compute
- Network
- Storage
- Billing
- Web

You have a virtual machine named ipslabvm that has the following configuration

- Private IP address - 10.104
- Network Security Group - ipslabnsg
- Public IP Address - None
- Subnet - 10.10.0/24
- Location - East US

You have to record all of the successful and failed connection attempts to the virtual machine
Which of the following actions would you implement for this requirement? Choose 3 answers from the options given below.

A. Ensure to register Microsoft. Insights resource provider
B. Ensure to add the Network Watcher connection monitor
C. Enable the Azure Network Watcher service in the East US region
D. Create a storage account
E. Enable the Azure Network Watcher flow logs

186. You have to create the Azure Kubernetes cluster. You need to complete the following Azure CLI script for this requirement.

```
Slot 1 create --name ipslabs-rg --location eastus
Slot 2 create --resource-group ipslabs-rg --name ipslabcluster --node-count 2
Slot 3 monitoring —generate-ssh-keys
```

Which of the following would go into Slot 1?

A. --enable-addons

B. az group

C. --create

D. az aks

187. You have to create the Azure Kubernetes cluster. You need to complete the following Azure CLI script for this requirement.

- Slot 1 create --name ipslabs-rg --location eastus
- Slot 2 create --resource-group ipslabs-rg --name ipslabcluster --node-count 2
- Slot 3 monitoring —generate-ssh-keys

Which of the following would go into Slot 2?

A. az group

B. --enable-addons

C. az aks

D. --create

188. The Azure Kubernetes cluster must be created. For this criterion, you must finish the Azure CLI script below.

- Slot 1 create --name ipslabs-rg --location eastus
- Slot 2 create --resource-group ipslabs-rg --name ipslabcluster --node-count 2
- Slot 3 monitoring —generate-ssh-keys

Which of the following would go into Slot 3?

A. --enable-addons

B. az group

C. aza ks

D. –create

189. Which of the following do you need to configure for ipslabgateway1?

A. Multi-site listener

B. AURL path-based routing rule

C. A basic routing rule
D. A basic listener

190. Which of the following do you need to configure for ipslabgateway2?

A. Multi-site
B. A basic listener
C. AURL path-based routing rule
D. A basic routing rule
E. Multi-site listeners

191. You have to implement the security objective for the below case study requirement. A storage account named ipslabappstore would be created. This storage account only needs to be accessed from the virtual network hosting the virtual machines. You decide to generate a shared access signature
Would this fulfill the requirement?

A. Yes
B. No

192. You have to implement the security objective for the below case study requirement. A storage account named ipslabappstore would be created. This storage account only needs to be accessed from the virtual network hosting the virtual machines. You decide to enable virtual network peering
Would this fulfill the requirement?

A. Yes
B. No

193. You have to implement the security objective for the below case study requirement. A storage account named ipslabappstore would be created. This storage account must only be accessed from the virtual network hosting the virtual machines. You decide to enable service endpoints
Would this fulfill the requirement?

A. Yes
B. No

194. Case Study.

Overview: IPS is an online training provider.
Existing Environment: The existing environment for IPS currently consists of the following resources in their on-premises data center. These resources are used for the daily operations of the various business units:

- File servers – Windows Server 2016
- Domain controllers – Windows Server 2012 R2
- Microsoft SQL Server servers - Windows Server 2016

The domain controllers support an Active Directory forest named ipslabs.com.
IPS also supports a web-based application called ips-app. Users across the world use this application. The application consists of the following tiers:

- A SQL database
- A web front end
- A processing middle tier

Following are the planned changes for IPS

- Migrate all ips-app tiers to Azure.
- Each tier would consist of 5 virtual machines.
- Users would access the web application tier using HTTPS only.
- Move the existing documents to Azure Blob storage using the internet.

Following are the technical requirements for IPS

- All Virtual machines hosted in Azure should be backed up.
- The documents in Azure BLOB storage should be stored in an archive storage tier.
- Azure AD should be used along with the on-premises Active Directory.
- Users should be synched between Azure AD and the on-premises Active Directory.
- User passwords or hashes should not be stored in Azure.
- When users join their own devices to Azure AD, they must use a phone verification method to verify their identity.
- There should be a pilot group so that the testing of devices joining Azure AD can be carried out.
- Administrative effort should be minimized whenever possible, and a mobile phone to verify their identity.
- A new user called ips-admin would be set as a service administrator of the Azure subscription.

The initial collection of papers has been asked to be moved to Azure. The documents have a total size of 500MB. Which of the following is the most appropriate implementation step to meet this requirement?

A. Generate a shared access signature (SAS). Map a drive and then copy the files by using File Explorer.
B. Generate an access key. Map a drive, and then copy the files by using File Explorer.
C. Use the Azure Import/Export service.
D. Use Azure Storage Explorer to copy the files.

195. Case Study.
Overview: IPS is an online training provider.
Existing Environment: The existing environment for IPS currently consists of the following resources in their on-premises data center. These resources are used for the daily operations of the various business units:

- File servers – Windows Server 2016
- Domain controllers – Windows Server 2012 R2
- Microsoft SQL Server servers - Windows Server 2016

The domain controllers support an Active Directory forest named ipslabs.com.
IPS also supports a web-based application called ips-app. Users across the world use this application. The application consists of the following tiers:

- A SQL database
- A web front end
- A processing middle tier

Following are the planned changes for IPS

- Migrate all ips-app tiers to Azure.
- Each tier would consist of 5 virtual machines.
- Users would access the web application tier using HTTPS only.
- Move the existing documents to Azure Blob storage using the internet.

Following are the technical requirements for IPS

- All Virtual machines hosted in Azure should be backed-up.
- The documents in Azure BLOB storage should be stored in an archive storage tier.
- Azure AD should be used along with the on-premises Active Directory.
- Users should be synched between Azure AD and the on-premises Active Directory.
- User passwords or hashes should not be stored in Azure.

- When users join their own devices to Azure AD, they need to use a phone verification method to verify their identity.
- There should be a pilot group so that the testing of devices joining Azure AD can be carried out.
- Administrative effort should be minimized whenever possible, and a mobile phone to verify their identity.
- A new user called ips-admin would be set as a service administrator of the Azure subscription.

The application ips-app is a critical application, therefore, you need to ensure a backup solution is in place for the application. Which of the following would need to be created first?

A. A recovery plan
B. A backup policy
C. An Azure Backup Server
D. A Recovery Services vault

196. Case Study.
Overview: IPS is an online training provider.
Existing Environment: The existing environment for IPS currently consists of the following resources in their on-premises data center. These resources are used for the daily operations of the various business units:

- File servers – Windows Server 2016
- Domain controllers – Windows Server 2012 R2
- Microsoft SQL Server servers - Windows Server 2016

The domain controllers support an Active Directory forest named ipslabs.com.
IPS also supports a web-based application called ips-app. Users across the world use this application. The application consists of the following tiers:

- A SQL database
- A web front end
- A processing middle tier

Following are the planned changes for IPS

- Migrate all ips-app tiers to Azure.
- Each tier would consist of 5 virtual machines.
- Users would access the web application tier using HTTPS only.
- Move the existing documents to Azure Blob storage using the internet.

Following are the technical requirements for IPS

- All Virtual machines hosted in Azure should be backed-up.
- The documents in Azure BLOB storage should be stored in an archive storage tier.
- Azure AD should be used along with the on-premises Active Directory.
- Users should be synched between Azure AD and the on-premises Active Directory.
- User passwords or hashes should not be stored in Azure.
- When users join their own devices to Azure AD, they need to use a phone verification method to verify their identity.
- There should be a pilot group so that the testing of devices joining Azure AD can be carried out.
- Administrative effort should be minimized whenever possible, and a mobile phone to verify their identity.
- A new user called ips-admin would be set as a service administrator of the Azure subscription.

You are working on the network design for hosting the different tiers of the IPS-app application. How many virtual networks would you recommend hosting the Virtual Machines for the application?

A. 1
B. 2
C. 3
D. 4

197. Case Study.
Overview: IPS is an online training provider.
Existing Environment: The existing environment for IPS currently consists of the following resources in their on-premises data center. These resources are used for the daily operations of the various business units:

- File servers – Windows Server 2016
- Domain controllers – Windows Server 2012 R2
- Microsoft SQL Server servers - Windows Server 2016

The domain controllers support an Active Directory forest named ipslabs.com.
IPS also supports a web-based application called ips-app. Users across the world use this application. The application consists of the following tiers:

- A SQL database
- A web front end
- A processing middle tier

Following are the planned changes for IPS

- Migrate all ips-app tiers to Azure.
- Each tier would consist of 5 virtual machines.
- Users would access the web application tier using HTTPS only.
- Move the existing documents to Azure Blob storage using the internet.

Following are the technical requirements for IPS

- All Virtual machines hosted in Azure should be backed-up.
- The documents in Azure BLOB storage should be stored in an archive storage tier.
- Azure AD should be used along with the on-premises Active Directory.
- Users should be synched between Azure AD and the on-premises Active Directory.
- User passwords or hashes should not be stored in Azure.
- When users join their own devices to Azure AD, they need to use a phone verification method to verify their identity.
- There should be a pilot group so that the testing of devices joining Azure AD can be carried out.
- Administrative effort should be minimized whenever possible, and a mobile phone to verify their identity.
- A new user called ips-admin would be set as a service administrator of the Azure subscription.

You are working on the network design for hosting the different tiers for the ips-app application. How many subnets would you recommend hosting the Virtual Machines for the application?

A. 1
B. 2
C. 3
D. 4

198. Case Study.
Overview: IPS is an online training provider.
Existing Environment: The existing environment for IPS currently consists of the following resources in their on-premises data center. These resources are used for the daily operations of the various business units:

- File servers – Windows Server 2016
- Domain controllers – Windows Server 2012 R2

- Microsoft SQL Server servers - Windows Server 2016

The domain controllers support an Active Directory forest named ipslabs.com.
IPS also supports a web-based application called ips-app. Users across the world use this application. The application consists of the following tiers:

- A SQL database
- A web front end
- A processing middle tier

Following are the planned changes for IPS

- Migrate all ips-app tiers to Azure.
- Each tier would consist of 5 virtual machines.
- Users would access the web application tier using HTTPS only.
- Move the existing documents to Azure Blob storage using the internet.

Following are the technical requirements for IPS

- All Virtual machines hosted in Azure should be backed-up.
- The documents in Azure BLOB storage should be stored in an archive storage tier.
- Azure AD should be used along with the on-premises Active Directory.
- Users should be synched between Azure AD and the on-premises Active Directory.
- User passwords or hashes should not be stored in Azure.
- When users join their own devices to Azure AD, they need to use a phone verification method to verify their identity.
- There should be a pilot group so that the testing of devices joining Azure AD can be carried out.
- Administrative effort should be minimized whenever possible, and a mobile phone to verify their identity.
- A new user called ips-admin would be set as a service administrator of the Azure subscription.

You need to ensure that users can join devices to Azure AD. But at the same time. You must ensure that the users only belong to the pilot Azure AD group.
Which of the two settings must you modify to implement this requirement?

A. Users may join devices to Azure AD Q
B. Additional local administrators on Azure AD joined devices
C. Users may register their devices with Azure AD
D. Require Multi-Factor Authentication to join devices

199. Case Study.

Overview: IPS is an online training provider.

Existing Environment: The existing environment for IPS currently consists of the following resources in their on-premises data center. These resources are used for the daily operations of the various business units:

- File servers – Windows Server 2016
- Domain controllers – Windows Server 2012 R2
- Microsoft SQL Server servers - Windows Server 2016

The domain controllers support an Active Directory forest named ipslabs.com.

IPS also supports a web-based application called ips-app. Users across the world use this application. The application consists of the following tiers:

- A SQL database
- A web front end
- A processing middle tier

Following are the planned changes for IPS

- Migrate all ips-app tiers to Azure.
- Each tier would consist of 5 virtual machines.
- Users would access the web application tier using HTTPS only.
- Move the existing documents to Azure Blob storage using the internet.

Following are the technical requirements for IPS

- All Virtual machines hosted in Azure should be backed-up.
- The documents in Azure BLOB storage should be stored in an archive storage tier.
- Azure AD should be used along with the on-premises Active Directory.
- Users should be synched between Azure AD and the on-premises Active Directory.
- User passwords or hashes should not be stored in Azure.
- When users join their own devices to Azure AD, they need to use a phone verification method to verify their identity.
- There should be a pilot group so that the testing of devices joining Azure AD can be carried out.
- Administrative effort should be minimized whenever possible, and a mobile phone to verify their identity.
- A new user called ips-admin would be set as a service administrator of the Azure subscription.

You are planning the move of the ips-app to Azure. You create a network security group (NSG). You need to recommend a solution to provide users with access to the ips-app. What should you recommend?

A. Create an outgoing security rule for port 443 from the Internet. Associate the Network Security Group with all the subnets.
B. Create an incoming security rule for port 443 from the Internet. Associate the Network Security Group with all the subnets.
C. Create an incoming security rule for port 443 from the Internet. Associate the Network Security Group to the subnet that contains the web "servers.
D. Create an outgoing security rule for port 443 from the Internet. Associate the Network Security Group to the subnet that contains the web "servers.

200. Your company has an on-premises file server named demo server that runs Windows Server 2016. Your company also has an Azure subscription that contains an Azure file share. You have to deploy an Azure File Sync Storage Sync Service. So you go ahead and create a sync group. You now need to synchronize files from the demo server to Azure. Which of the following actions would you need to perform for this purpose? Choose 3 answers from the options given below.

A. Create an Azure on-premises data gateway
B. Install the Azure File Sync agent on the demo server
C. Create a Recovery Services vault
D. Register demo server
E. Install the DFS Replication server role on the demo server
F. Add a server endpoint

201. Your company has an Azure subscription that is used by multiple departments in your company. The subscription contains around § resource groups. Each department uses resources in several resource groups. Your supervisor has requested to send a report that details the costs for each department. Which of the following actions would you need to perform for this purpose? Choose 3 answers from the options given below.

A. Assign a tag to each resource group
B. Use the Resource costs blade of each resource group
C. Download the usage report
D. Assign a tag to each resource
E. From the Costs Analysis blade, filter the view by tag

202. You have an Azure Active Directory (Azure AD) tenant with the initial domain name. You have a domain name of ips.com registered at a third-party registrar. You

need to ensure that you can create Azure AD users that have names containing a suffix of aips.com.
Which of the following would need to be implemented to fulfill this requirement? Choose 3 answers from the options given below.

A. Configure the company branding
B. Add an Azure AD tenant
C. Verify the domain
D. Create an Azure DNS Zone
E. Add a custom domain name
F. Add a record to the public ips.com DNS zone

203. An Azure account and subscription are currently in use by a corporation. They want to use Virtual Machines and a load balancer to host an application. It is necessary to ensure that the application is available 99.99 percent of the time. Which of the following would have to be in place in order for this to work? You must also keep the solution's costs to a minimum. Choose two responses from the list below.

A. Create a Basic Load balancer
B. Create a Standard Load balancer
C. Add 2 Virtual Machines to the backend pool
D. Add a Virtual Machine to the backend pool

204. A corporation has set up a load balancer that distributes traffic across three virtual servers on ports 80 and 443. You must direct all RDP traffic to a virtual machine called demovm. How would you go about accomplishing this?

A. By creating a new public load balancer for demovm
B. By creating a new internal load balancer for demovm
C. By creating an inbound NAT rule
D. By creating a new IP configuration

205. A corporation has set up a load balancer that distributes traffic across three virtual servers on ports 80 and 443. For each request, you must ensure that all clients are served by the same web server. Which of the following would you set up to meet this need?

A. Floating IP
B. Health Probe
C. Session Persistence
D. TCP Reset

206. A business has begun to use Azure and has established a subscription. They want to see the costs associated with each resource type. Which of the following will assist you in obtaining these details?

A. Go to your Azure AD directory and go to Cost Analysis
B. Go to your Subscription and go to Cost Analysis
C. Go to your Subscription and go to Resource Groups
D. Go to your Azure AD directory and go to Licenses

207. In Azure, your firm already has a Virtual Network defined. A default subnet in the Virtual Network has two virtual machines named demovm and demovm1. For a period of three hours, all network traffic between the Virtual Machines must be examined. You provide a method for creating a Data Collector collection.
Does this solution fulfill the requirement?

A. Yes
B. No

208. In Azure, your firm already has a Virtual Network defined. A default subnet in the Virtual Network has two virtual machines named demovm and demovm1. For a period of three hours, all network traffic between the Virtual Machines must be examined. You suggest an Azure Network Watcher Packet Capture solution.
Does this solution fulfill the requirement?

A. Yes
B. No

209. In Azure, your firm already has a Virtual Network defined. A default subnet in the Virtual Network has two virtual machines named demovm and demovm1. For a period of three hours, all network traffic between the Virtual Machines must be examined. You offer a method for creating a network in and network out metric chart.
Does this solution fulfill the requirement?

A. Yes
B. No

210. You are the Azure administrator for a company. You must create a custom role based on the Virtual Machine Reader role. You have to complete the following PowerShell script.

```
$ipsrole = SLOT 1 "Virtual Machine Reader"
$ ipsrole.id = $null
$ ipsrole.Name = "Virtual Machine Reader"
$ ipsrole.Description = "Read permissions for virtual machines"
$ ipsrole.Actions.Clear()
$ ipsrole.Actions.Add("Microsoft.Storage/*/read")
$ ipsrole.Actions.Add("Microsoft.Network/*/read")
$ ipsrole.Actions.Add("Microsoft.Compute/*/read")
$ ipsrole.AssignableScopes.Clear()
$ ipsrole.AssignableScopes.Add("/subscriptions/000230400-0500-0440-0440-0055500000000")
SLOT2-Role $ipsrole
```

Which of the following would come in Slot 1?

A. Get-AzRoleDefinition
B. Set-AzRoleDefinition
C. New-AzRoleDefinition
D. Create-AzRoleDefinition

211. You are the Azure administrator for a company. You must create a custom role based on the Virtual Machine Reader role. You have to complete the following PowerShell script.

```
$ipsrole = SLOT 1 "Virtual Machine Reader"
$ ipsrole.id = $null
$ ipsrole.Name = "Virtual Machine Reader"
$ ipsrole.Description = "Read permissions for virtual machines"
```

```
$ ipsrole.Actions.Clear()
$ ipsrole.Actions.Add("Microsoft.Storage/*/read")
$ ipsrole.Actions.Add("Microsoft.Network/*/read")
$ ipsrole.Actions.Add("Microsoft.Compute/*/read")
$ ipsrole.AssignableScopes.Clear()
$ ipsrole.AssignableScopes.Add("/subscriptions/000230400-0500-0440-0440-0055500000000")
SLOT2-Role $ipsrole
```

Which of the following would come in Slot 2?

A. Get-AzRoleDefinition
B. New-AzRoleDefinition
C. Create-AzRoleDefinition
D. Set-AzRoleDefinition

212. A business has just set up an Azure account and subscription. It is required that IT administrators only be able to create virtual machines of a specific SKU size. Which of the following can assist you in achieving this goal?

A. Create an RBAC role and assign it to the relevant resource group
B. Create an Azure policy and assign it to the subscription
C. Assign the appropriate subscription policy to the IT administrators' group
D. Assign the appropriate AD role to the IT administrators' group

213. A company has the following set of Virtual Machines defined in the Azure account.

Name	Region
ips-vm1	East US
ips=vm2	Central US

The company wants to move ips-vm1 to another subscription. Which of the following can be implemented to fulfill this requirement?

A. Move the Virtual Machine to the Central US region first

B. You cannot move the Virtual Machine across subscriptions. You would need to delete and recreate the VM in the new subscription
C. Use the Move-AZ Resource PowerShell command to move the Virtual Machine
D. Use the Move-Resource PowerShell command to move the Virtual Machine

214. A team has a Virtual Machine defined in Azure. A new network interface named secondary has been created. The Network interface needs to be added to the Virtual machine. What needs to be done initially to make sure the virtual machine can attach to the network interface?

A. The machine needs to be stopped first.
B. The Network security group rules need to be removed from the network interface
C. The primary network interface needs to be removed
D. The public IP needs to be deallocated from the primary network interface

215. A company has the following virtual networks defined in Azure.

Name	Address space
ips-network1	10,1.0.0/16
ips-network2	10.2.0.0/16

The following virtual machines have been defined as well.

Name	Network
ipsvm1	ips-network1
ipsvm2	ips-network2

The necessary peering connections have been created between ips-network1 and ips-network2. The firewalls on the virtual machines have been modified to allow ICMP traffic. But traffic does not seem to flow between the virtual machines when the ping request is made.
Which of the following can be used to diagnose the issue?

A. Application Insights
B. IP Flow Verify
C. Azure Security Center

D. Azure Advisor

216. A company has the following virtual networks defined in Azure.

Name	Address space
ips-network1	10,1.0.0/16
ips-network2	10.2.0.0/16

The following virtual machines have been defined as well.

Name	Network
ipsvm1	ips-network1
ipsvm2	ips-network2

The required peering connections have been created between ips-network1 and ips-network2. The firewalls on the virtual machines have been modified to allow ICMP traffic. But traffic does not seem to flow between the virtual machines when the ping request is made.
If the security department wanted to check on any network intrusions into the virtual networks, which of the following tool could be used for this purpose?
Which of the following can be used to diagnose the issue?

A. IP Flow Verify
B. Variable packet capture
C. Application Insights
D. Azure connection monitor

217. Your company has an Azure account and subscription. The subscription contains a virtual machine named demovm. You have a computer named Computer1 that runs Windows 10. Computer1 is connected to the Internet. You add a network interface to the VM1 from Computer. You attempt to connect to demovm by using Remote Desktop, but the connection fails. You need to establish a Remote Desktop connection to demovm.
What should you do first?

A. Start demovm.
B. Delete the DenyAllOutBound outbound port rule.

C. Attach a network interface.
D. Delete the DenyAllinBound inbound port rule.

218. Your company has an Azure account and subscription. The subscription contains a virtual machine named demovm. You have a computer named Computer1 that runs Windows 10. The computer is connected to the Internet. You add a network interface to the VM1 from Computer1; you want to be able to also access a web service running on port 80 after demovm is started.
Which of the following must be done for this to work?

A. Attach a network interface.
B. Add an incoming network security group rule for allowing traffic on port 80
C. Delete the DenyAllOutBound outbound port rule.
D. Add an outgoing network security group rule for allowing traffic on port 80
E. Delete the DenyAllinBound inbound port rule.

219. Your company has an Azure account and subscription. The subscription contains the resources in the following table:

Name	Type
ipsstore	Storage container
ips-rg	Resource Group
documents	BLOB container
demo	File share

Using a single Azure Resource Manager template, your IT administrator created a virtual machine called demovm and a storage account called ips-temp. You should go over the template that was used for the deployment again. To access the template that was used for the deployment, which of the following resource blades should be used?

A. ips-rg
B. demovm
C. ipsstore
D. ips-temp

220. Your company has an Azure subscription. In the subscription. You go ahead and create an Azure file snare named share1. You also create a shared access signature (SAS) named SASdemo. If you use SASdemo to connect to the storage

account and open Microsoft Azure Storage Explorer on a machine with an IP address of 193.77.134.1, then you:

A. Will be prompted for the credentials
B. Will have read, write, and list access
C. Will have no access
D. Will have read-only access

221. Your company has an Azure subscription. You go ahead and create an Azure file share named share1. You also create a shared access signature (SAS) named SASdemo. If you use the net, use the command on a computer with an IP address of 193.77.134.50 and then use SASdemo to connect to share1. Then you......

A. Will have no access
B. Will be prompted for the credentials
C. Will have read, write, and list access
D. Will have read-only access

222. You want to set up a virtual network subnet with five virtual machines. A public IP address and a private IP address will be assigned to each virtual machine. Inbound and outbound security policies must be the same for each virtual machine.
What is the bare minimum of network interfaces you need?

A. 5
B. 10
C. 15
D. 20

223. You want to set up a virtual network subnet with five virtual machines. A public IP address and a private IP address will be assigned to each virtual machine. Inbound and outbound security policies must be the same for each virtual machine.
What is the bare minimum of network security groups you need?

A. 1
B. 2
C. 5
D. 10

224. You have a virtual network named VNet2 that has the configuration.

```
Name                   : VNET2
ResourceGroupName      : demonew
Location               : uksouth
Id                     : /subscriptions/baaa99b3-1d19-4c5e-90e1-39d55de5fc6e/resourceGroups/d
                         emonew/providers/Microsoft.Network/virtualNetworks/VNET2
Etag                   : W/"b0b5ef85-4e7e-4d99-a2be-16f35e4fdc0a"
ResourceGuid           : 164448dd-357b-4c2b-8762-885ef8e90084
ProvisioningState      : Succeeded
Tags                   :
AddressSpace           : {
                           "AddressPrefixes": [
                             "10.2.0.0/16"
                           ]
                         }
DhcpOptions            : {}
Subnets                : [
                           {
                             "Name": "default",
                             "Etag": "W/\"b0b5ef85-4e7e-4d99-a2be-16f35e4fdc0a\"",
                             "Id": "/subscriptions/baaa99b3-1d19-4c5e-90e1-39d55de5fc6e/resou
                         rceGroups/demonew/providers/Microsoft.Network/virtualNetworks/VNET2/
                         subnets/default",
                             "AddressPrefix": "10.2.0.0/24",
                             "IpConfigurations": [],
                             "ResourceNavigationLinks": [],
                             "ServiceEndpoints": [],
                             "ProvisioningState": "Succeeded"
                           }
                         ]
VirtualNetworkPeerings : []
EnableDdosProtection   : false
DdosProtectionPlan     : null
```

Before a virtual machine on VNET2 can receive an IP address from 192 168.1.0/24, you must first.

A. Add a network interface
B. Add a subnet
C. Add an address space go
D. Delete an address space
E. Delete a subnet

225. You have a virtual network named VNet2 that has the configuration.

```
Name                   : VNET2
ResourceGroupName      : demonew
Location               : uksouth
Id                     : /subscriptions/baaa99b3-1d19-4c5e-90e1-39d55de5fc6e/resourceGroups/d
                         emonew/providers/Microsoft.Network/virtualNetworks/VNET2
Etag                   : W/"b0b5ef85-4e7e-4d99-a2be-16f35e4fdc0a"
ResourceGuid           : 164448dd-357b-4c2b-8762-885ef8e90084
ProvisioningState      : Succeeded
Tags                   :
AddressSpace           : {
                           "AddressPrefixes": [
                             "10.2.0.0/16"
                           ]
                         }
DhcpOptions            : {}
Subnets                : [
                           {
                             "Name": "default",
                             "Etag": "W/\"b0b5ef85-4e7e-4d99-a2be-16f35e4fdc0a\"",
                             "Id": "/subscriptions/baaa99b3-1d19-4c5e-90e1-39d55de5fc6e/resou
                         rceGroups/demonew/providers/Microsoft.Network/virtualNetworks/VNET2/
                         subnets/default",
                             "AddressPrefix": "10.2.0.0/24",
                             "IpConfigurations": [],
                             "ResourceNavigationLinks": [],
                             "ServiceEndpoints": [],
                             "ProvisioningState": "Succeeded"
                           }
                         ]
VirtualNetworkPeerings : []
EnableDdosProtection   : false
DdosProtectionPlan     : null
```

Before a virtual machine on VNET2 can receive an IP address from 10 2.1.0/24, you must first,

A. Add a network interface
B. Add a subnet
C. Add an address space
D. Delete an address space
E. Delete a subnet

226. A company has an Azure subscription that contains the resources in the following table:

Name	Type
ips-rg	Resource Group
ipsstore	Azure Storage account
iipssync	Azure File Sync

The ipsstore contains a file share named documents. The document file share contains 1000 files.

You need to synchronize the files in the file share with an on-premises server named ipsserver. Which of the following would you need to implement to fulfill this requirement? Choose 3 answers from the options given below.

A. Download an automation script.
B. Create a container instance.
C. Create a sync group.
D. Register ipsserver.
E. Install the Azure File Sync agent on ipsserver.

227. A company needs to create a storage account that needs to conform to the following requirements

- Users should be able to add files such as images and videos
- Ability to store archive data
- File shares need to be in place which can be accessed across several VMs
- The data needs to be available even if a region goes down
- The solution needs to be cost-effective

Which of the following type of storage accounts would you create for this purpose?

A. BLOB storage
B. General Purpose(v1)
C. General Purpose(v2)
D. Table storage

228. A company needs to create a storage account that needs to conform to the following requirements

- Users should be able to add files such as images and videos
- Ability to store archive data
- File shares need to be in place which can be accessed across several VMs
- The data needs to be available even if a region goes down
- The solution needs to be cost-effective

What is the type of replication that needs to be configured for the storage account?

A. Zone-redundant storage (ZRS)
B. Locally redundant storage (LRS)
C. Geo-redundant storage (GRS)
D. Read-access geo-redundant storage (RA-GRS)

229. You must deploy two Azure virtual machines named VM1 and VM2 based on the Windows server 2016. The deployment must meet the following requirements:

- Provide a Service Level Agreement (SLA) of 99.95 percent availability.
- Use managed disks
- You propose a solution to create a scale set for the requirement.

Would the solution meet the goal?

A. Yes
B. No

230. You must deploy two Azure virtual machines named VM1 and VM2 based on the Windows server 2016 image. The deployment must meet the following requirements:

- Provide a Service Level Agreement (SLA) of 99.95 percent availability.
- Use managed disks
- You propose a solution to create an availability set for the requirement.

Would the solution meet the goal?

A. Yes
B. No

231. You must deploy two Azure virtual machines named VM1 and VM2 based on the Windows server 2016. The deployment must meet the following requirements:

- Provide a Service Level Agreement (SLA) of 99.95 percent availability.
- Use managed disks
- You propose a solution to create a Traffic Manager for the requirement.

Would the solution meet the goal?

A. Yes
B. No

232. Your company has an Azure account and an Azure subscription. They have created a Virtual Network named ips-net. The following users have been set up.

User	Role

ips-usr1	Owner
ips-usr2	Security admin
ips-usr3	Network Contributor

Which of the following users would be able to add a subnet to the Virtual Network?

A. ips-usr1 only
B. ips-usr2 only
C. ips-usr3 only
D. ips-usr1 and ips-usr2 only
E. ips-usr1 and ips-usr3 only
F. ips-usr2 and ips-usr3 only
G. ips-usr1, ips-usr2 and ips-usr3

233. Your company has an Azure account and an Azure subscription. They have created a Virtual Network named ips-net. The following users have been set up.

User	Role
ips-usr1	Owner
ips-usr2	Security admin
ips-usr3	Network Contributor

Which of the following users would be able to add the Reader role access for a user to the Virtual Network?

A. ips-usr1 only
B. ips-usr2 only
C. ips-usr3 only
D. ips-usr1 and ips-usr2 only
E. ips-usr1 and ips-usr3 only
F. ips-usr2 and ips-usr3 only
G. ips-usr1, ips-usr2 and ips-usr3

234. You work as an Azure Administrator for a company. You have the below JSON role definition.

```
{
  "assignableScopes": [
    "/"
  ],
  "description": "Lets you create and manage Support requests",
  "id": "/subscriptions/{subscriptionId}/providers/Microsoft.Authorization/roleDefinitions/cfd33db0-3dd1-45e3-aa9d-cdbdf3b6f24e",
  "name": "cfd33db0-3dd1-45e3-aa9d-cdbdf3b6f24e",
  "permissions": [
    {
      "actions": [
        SLOT 1,
        "Microsoft.Resources/subscriptions/resourceGroups/read",
        SLOT 2
      ],
      "notActions": [],
      "dataActions": [],
      "notDataActions": []
    }
  ],
  "roleName": "Support Request Contributor",
  "roleType": "BuiltInRole",
  "type": "Microsoft.Authorization/roleDefinitions"
}
```

You have to ensure that a role can be in place that would have the following requirements.

- View all the resources in the Azure subscription
- Issue support requests to Microsoft.
- Use the principle of least privilege.
- You have to complete the below JSON role definition

Which of the following would go into Slot1?

A. "Microsoft.Authorization/*/"
B. "Microsoft.Authorization/*/read"
C. " Microsoft.Authorization/read/"
D. "Microsoft.Authorization/"

235. You work as an Azure Administrator for a company. You have the below JSON role definition.

```
{
  "assignableScopes": [
    "/"
  ],
  "description": "Lets you create and manage Support requests",
  "id": "/subscriptions/{subscriptionId}/providers/Microsoft.Authorization/roleDefinitions/cfd33db0-3dd1-45e3-aa9d-cdbdf3b6f24e",
  "name": "cfd33db0-3dd1-45e3-aa9d-cdbdf3b6f24e",
  "permissions": [
    {
      "actions": [
        SLOT 1,
        "Microsoft.Resources/subscriptions/resourceGroups/read",
        SLOT 2
      ],
      "notActions": [],
      "dataActions": [],
      "notDataActions": []
    }
  ],
  "roleName": "Support Request Contributor",
  "roleType": "BuiltInRole",
  "type": "Microsoft.Authorization/roleDefinitions"
}
```

You have to ensure that a role can be in place that would have the following requirements.

- View all the resources in the Azure subscription
- Issue support requests to Microsoft.
- Use the principle of least privilege
- You have to complete the below JSON role definition

Which of the following would go into Slot2?

A. "*/*"
B. "*/Microsoft.Support
C. "Microsoft.Support/"
D. "Microsoft.Support"

236. You have the Azure virtual networks shown in the following table.

Name	Address space	Subnet	Resource group-region
VNet1	10.11,0.0/16	10.11.0.0/17	West US
VNet2	10.11.0.0/17	10.11.0.0/25	West US
VNet3	10.10.0.0/22	10.0.1.0/24	East US
VNet4	192.168 16.0/22	192.168 16.0/24	North Europe

To which virtual networks can you establish a peering connection from VNet1?

A. VNet2 and VNet3 only
B. VNetz2 only
C. VNet3 and VNet4 only
D. VNet2, VNet3, and VNet4

237. Your company has an Azure account and a subscription. The subscription contains the virtual networks in the following table.

Name	Address space	Subnet name	Subnet address range

VNet1	10.1.0.0/16	Subnet1	10.1.1.0/24
VNet2	10.10.0.0/16	Subnet2	10.10.1.0/24
VNet3	172.16.0.0/16	Subnet3	172.16.L0/24

The virtual machines listed in the table are also included in the subscription.

Name	Network	Subnet	IP address
VM1	VNet1	Subnet1	10,1.1.4
VM2	VNet2	Subnet2	10.1014
VM3	VNet3	Subnet3	172.16.1.4

All virtual machines' firewalls are set to allow all ICMP traffic. The peerings are entered in the table below.

Virtual network	Peering network
VNet1	VNet3
VNet2	VNet3
VNet3	VNet1

For each of the following statements. Select Yes if the statement is true
Does VM1 peer with VM3?

A. Yes
B. No

238. Your company has an Azure account and a subscription. The subscription contains the virtual networks in the following table.

Name	Address space	Subnet name	Subnet address range
VNet1	10.1.0.0/16	Subnet1	10.1.1.0/24
VNet2	10.10.0.0/16	Subnet2	10.10.1.0/24
VNet3	172.16.0.0/16	Subnet3	172.16.L0/24

The subscription also contains the virtual machines in the following table.

Name	Network	Subnet	IP address
VM1	VNet1	Subnet1	10,1.1.4
VM2	VNet2	Subnet2	10.1014
VM3	VNet3	Subnet3	172.16.1.4

All virtual machines' firewalls are set to allow all ICMP traffic. The peerings are entered in the table below.

Virtual network	Peering network
VNet1	VNet3
VNet2	VNet3
VNet3	VNet1

For each of the following statements, select yes, if the statement is true.
Does VM2 peer with VM3?

A. Yes
B. No

239. Your company has an Azure account and a subscription. The subscription contains the virtual networks in the following table.

Name	Address space	Subnet name	Subnet address range
VNet1	10.1.0.0/16	Subnet1	10.1.1.0/24
VNet2	10.10.0.0/16	Subnet2	10.10.1.0/24
VNet3	172.16.0.0/16	Subnet3	172.16.L0/24

The subscription also contains the virtual machines in the following table.

Name	Network	Subnet	IP address
VM1	VNet1	Subnet1	10,1.1.4
VM2	VNet2	Subnet2	10.1014
VM3	VNet3	Subnet3	172.16.1.4

All virtual machines' firewalls are set to allow all ICMP traffic. The peerings are entered in the table below.

Virtual network	Peering network
VNet1	VNet3
VNet2	VNet3
VNet3	VNet1

For each of the following statements. Select Yes, if the statement is true.
Does VM2 peer with VM1?

A. Yes
B. No

240. The following storage accounts are available as part of a company's Azure subscription.

Name	Storage account type
ipsstore1	General Purpose V1
ipsstore2	General Purpose V2
ipsstore3	Blob Storage

Which storage account(s) could be utilized to store things in the Archive tier?

A. ipsstore1 only
B. ipsstore2 only
C. ipsstore3 only
D. ipsstore1 and ipsstore2 only
E. ipsstore1 and ipsstore3 only
F. ipsstore2 and ipsstore3 only
G. All storage accounts

241. A company needs to deploy the following architecture to Azure.
The architecture would consist of a load balancer that should only accept requests via private IP addresses and should not flow via the internet. The load balancer would direct requests to database servers hosted on Virtual machines.

For this architecture, which of the following load balancer types should be used?

A. Private Load balancer
B. Public Load balancer
C. Internal Load balancer
D. External Load balancer

242. Case Study.
Overview: IPS is an online training provider.
Existing Environment: The existing environment for IPS currently consists of the following:

- A set of Virtual machines that host web-based application workloads
- A set of Virtual machines that host database workloads
- An Active directory setup using Windows Server 2012 R2

Proposed Environment

- IPS has set up an Azure Active Directory (Azure AD) tenant recently
- They want to migrate their web and database workloads to the cloud
- They also want to set up a document store where users will be able to upload and download files

Infrastructure changes

- There is a need to set up Azure AD and ensure users from their on-premises Active directory are synced up to Azure AD
- A custom domain of ips.com also needs to be set up in Azure
- The web-based Virtual Machines in Azure should only allow HTTPS traffic for the Internet-based users
- Non-Functional requirements
- An SLA of 99.5% needs to be guaranteed for the availability of the Virtual Machines
- Storage replication needs to be in place to ensure that data is available even in the case of a data center failure
- Wherever possible, costs should be minimized.

Which of the following should be used to ensure an SLA of 99.5% for the availability of the Virtual Machines? Choose 2 answers from the options given below.

A. Azure Managed Disks
B. Azure Network Interfaces
C. Azure Availability sets

D. Azure scale sets

243. Case Study

Overview: IPS is an online training provider.

Existing Environment: The existing environment for IPS currently consists of the following:

- A set of Virtual machines that host web-based application workloads
- A set of Virtual machines that host database workloads
- An Active directory setup using Windows Server 2012 R2

Proposed Environment

- IPS has set up an Azure Active Directory (Azure AD) tenant recently
- They want to migrate their web and database workloads to the cloud
- They also want to set up a document store where users will be able to upload and download files

Infrastructure changes

- There is a need to set up Azure AD and ensure users from their on-premises Active directory are synced up to Azure AD
- A custom domain of ips.com also needs to be set up in Azure
- The web-based Virtual Machines in Azure should only allow HTTPS traffic for the Internet-based users
- Non-Functional requirements
- An SLA of 99.5% needs to be guaranteed for the availability of the Virtual Machines
- Storage replication needs to be in place to ensure that data is available even in the case of a data center failure

Wherever possible, costs should be minimized when adding custom domain names. Which of the following record needs to be added to your custom domain registrar?

A. NS record
B. A record
C. TXT record
D. PTR record

244. Case Study

Overview: IPS is an online training provider.

Existing Environment: The existing environment for IPS currently consists of the following:

- A set of Virtual machines that host web-based application workloads

- A set of Virtual machines that host database workloads
- An Active directory setup using Windows Server 2012 R2

Proposed Environment

- IPS has set up an Azure Active Directory (Azure AD) tenant recently
- They want to migrate their web and database workloads to the cloud
- They also want to set up a document store where users will be able to upload and download files

Infrastructure changes

- There is a need to set up Azure AD and ensure users from their on-premises Active Directory are synced up to Azure AD
- A custom domain of ips.com also needs to be set up in Azure
- The web-based Virtual Machines in Azure should only allow HTTPS traffic for the Internet-based users

Non-Functional requirements

- An SLA of 99.5% needs to be guaranteed for the availability of the Virtual Machines
- Storage replication needs to be in place to ensure that data is available even in the case of a data center failure
- Wherever possible, costs should be minimized.

Which of the following rule would you apply to the Network Security Group for the Network interface attached to the webserver?

A. An inbound rule allowing traffic on port 80
B. An inbound rule allowing traffic on port 443
C. An outbound rule allowing traffic on port 443
D. An outbound rule allowing traffic on port 80

245. A team member has created a point-to-site VPN connection between a computer named "WorkstationA" and an Azure Virtual Network. Another point-to-site VPN connection needs to be created between the same Azure Virtual Network and a computer named "WorkstationB". The VPN client package was generated and installed on "WorkstationB". You need to ensure you can create a successful point-to-site VPN connection. You make the decision to join "WorkstationB" with the Azure AD tenant.
Would this solution fulfill the requirement?

A. Yes
B. No

246. A team member has established a point-to-site VPN connection between an Azure Virtual Network and a PC named "WorkstationA." A point-to-site VPN connection between the same Azure Virtual Network and a PC named "WorkstationB" must be established. On "WorkstationB," a VPN client package was created and installed. You need to ensure you can create a successful point-to-site VPN connection. You make the decision to create a local VPN gateway.
Would this solution fulfill the requirement?

A. Yes
B. No

247. Azure Active Directory (Azure AD) and Microsoft 365 tenants for your business go by the moniker contoso.com. The business makes use of numerous Azure Files directories. A distinct division is assigned to each share of the company. In Azure AD, the department property contains information on every person.

The division file shares must be accessible to the users. The solution should demand the least quantity of administrative effort.

Which two categories of organizations should you employ? Each correct answer offers a complete resolution.

A. A security group with dynamic enrollment

B. A club in Microsoft 365 that makes use of the dynamic membership type

C. The delivery squad

D. A security organization utilizing the specified membership type

E. A group in Microsoft 365 that makes use of the designated membership category

248. You have a client called contoso.com in Azure Active Directory (Azure AD).

You must ensure that User1 has access to the tenant's entire collection of settings but cannot change any settings.

Which position should you give User1?

A. Directory Readers

B. Security Reader

C. Reports Reader

D. Global Reader

249. You have a tenant called contoso.com in your operational Azure Active Directory (Azure AD).

You launch a development Azure Active Directory (AD) tenant, giving the development tenant several unique administrative roles.

The responsibilities must be copied to the production tenant.

What should you start with?

A. Export the custom responsibilities to JSON from the development tenant

B. Create a new custom job from the production tenant

C. Run a backup from the production tenant

D. Create an administrative entity from the production tenant

250. You have many virtual computers in your Azure subscription. You want to make an Azure Monitor action rule that gets triggered after five minutes of a virtual computer using more than 80% of its processor resources.

The recipient of the action rule notice must be specified.

What should you produce?

A. Action Group

B. Security Group

C. Distribution Group

D. Microsoft 365 Group

251. There are ten distinct divisions in your business.

You have a large number of virtual computers in your Azure subscription. Only the virtual computers used by their respective departments are used by users.

The virtual machines will receive resource tags specific to each section from you.

Which two options should you choose? Each correct answer offers a complete resolution.

A. PowerShell

B. Azure Resource Manager (ARM) Templates

C. App Registrations

D. Azure Advisor

252. The storage accounts listed in the accompanying table are part of your Azure subscription.

Name	Kind	Performance	Replication

Storage1	StorageV2 (general purpose v2)	Standard	Zone-redundant storage (ZRS)
Storage2	BloblStorage	Standard	Locally-redundant storage (LRS)
Storage3	FileStorage	Premium	Zone-redundant storage (ZRS)
Storage4	Storage (general purpose v1)	premium	Locally-redundant storage (LRS)

Which storage accounts can be converted to Geo-Redundant Storage (GRS) must be determined.

Which storage locations should be noted down?

A. Storage1 only

B. Storage2 only

C. Storage3 only

D. Storage4 only

E. Storage1 and Storage4 only

F. Storage2 and Storage3 only

253. You have a Azure subscription.

You intend to use an Azure Resource Manager (ARM) template to launch numerous Azure virtual machines.

The credentials that will be used for the deployment need to be stored safely.

Which of the following should you employ?

A. Identity Protection with Azure Active Directory (Azure AD)

B. Azure Key Vault

C. Azure Storage Account

D. Azure Encryption Scopes

254. You have several empty resources in a resource group called RG1.

To remove RG1 and all of its resources without requesting approval, you must use the Azure CLI.

Which instruction should you enter?

A. group remove --name rg1 --no-wait az --yes

B. group deployment remove with the options rg1 and no-wait

C. az group update --name rg1 --remove

D. az group wait –deleted –resource-group rg1

255. You have VM1, a virtual computer in Azure.

The same configurations as VM1 must be used to make five more virtual machines. The solution must ensure that VM1 is always reachable.

You access the blade for VM1 from the Azure portal.

What should you do now?

A. Select Capture

B. Select availability and scaling

C. Select Redeploy + reapply

D. Select an Export template

256. You have an Azure membership with the web app webapp1 from the Azure App Service. The domain name for Webapp1 is webapp1.azurewebsites.net.

You must update webapp1 to include a unique URL called http://www.contoso.com.

You check who owns the name.

Which of the following DNS entries should you use?

A. SRV

B. CNAME

C. TXT

D. PTR

257. You have a virtual computer called VM1 in your Azure subscription.

Volume encryption is necessary for VM1's operating system and data discs.

You make vault1 the name of an Azure key vault.

You must configure vault1 to make Azure Disk Encryption available for disc encryption.

Which option for vault1 should you change?

A. Keys

B. Secrets

C. Access policies

D. Security

258. The resources listed in the accompanying table are part of your Azure subscription.

Name	Description
VM1	Azure Virtual Machine
blob1	Azure Blob Storage
Disk1	Azure Disk
share1	Azure File Storage
Database1	Azure Database for PostgreSQL servers

What two tools can be backed up to a Recovery Services vault? Each correct answer reveals a piece of the solution.

A. VM1

B. blob1

C. Disk1

D. share1

E. Database1

259. Your business has several divisions. There are numerous Virtual Machines (VMs) in each area.

The business has a resource group called RG1 in its Azure contract.

RG1 is the location of all VMs.

How would you ensure each VM is connected to the appropriate section?

A. Establish Azure Management Groups for every division

B. Establish a support club for each department

C. Assign tags to the virtual machines

D. Modify the settings of the virtual machines

260. You intend to add an Ubuntu Server virtual server to the Azure subscription of your business.

It would help if you performed a particular deployment involving adding a trusted root Certification Authority (CA).

Which of the following should be used to build the virtual machine?

A. The New-AzureRmVm cmdlet

B. The New-AzVM cmdlet

C. The Create-AzVM cmdlet

D. The az VM creates a command

261. When employees are absent in the office, your business uses multi-factor authentication. The usage paradigm has been set to the Per Authentication option.

After purchasing a subsidiary company and adding the new staff to Azure Active Directory (Azure AD), you are told that these employees should also use Multi-Factor Authentication.

To achieve this, the Per Enabled User setting for the usage model must be specified.

Solution: You can modify the current usage paradigm using the Azure portal.

Is the approach achieving the goal?

A. Yes

B. No

262. Your company's Azure solution uses multi-factor authentication when users are not in the workplace. The usage paradigm has been set to the Per Authentication option.

After purchasing a subsidiary company and adding the new staff to Azure Active Directory (Azure AD), you are told that these employees should also use Multi-Factor Authentication.

To achieve this, the Per Enabled User setting for the usage model must be specified.

Solution: You can modify the current usage paradigm using the Azure CLI.

Is the approach achieving the goal?

A. Yes

B. No

263. Your company's Azure solution uses multi-factor authentication when users are not in the workplace. The usage paradigm has been set to the Per Authentication option.

After purchasing a subsidiary company and adding the new staff to Azure Active Directory (Azure AD), you are told that these employees should also use Multi-Factor Authentication.

To achieve this, the Per Enabled User setting for the usage model must be specified.

Solution: You back up the data from the current Multi-Factor Authentication provider and use it to establish a new Multi-Factor Authentication provider.

Is the approach achieving the goal?

A. Yes

B. No

264. Your business is a subscriber to Microsoft Azure.

The business maintains data centers in New York and Los Angeles.

For site resilience, you are setting up the two data centers as geo-clustered sites.

You must suggest a redundant Azure storage solution to store the data with the following features:

- Data must be kept across multiple servers
- Data must be kept on servers located in different regions
- Both the central location and the secondary site can read data

Which choice for Azure stored redundancy should be suggested?

A. Geo-Redundant Storage

B. Read-Only Geo-Redundant Storage

C. Zone-Redundant Storage

D. Locally Redundant Storage

265. Your business's Azure membership includes a storage account, resource group, blob container, and file share.

Coworker Jon Ross installs a virtual machine and an extra Azure Storage account using a single Azure Resource Manager (ARM) template.

The ARM blueprint that Jon Ross used should be examined.

Solution: Access the blade for the virtual machine.

Is the approach achieving the goal?

A. Yes

B. No

266. Your business's Azure membership includes a storage account, resource group, blob container, and file share.

Coworker Jon Ross installs a virtual machine and an extra Azure Storage account using a single Azure Resource Manager (ARM) template.

The ARM blueprint that Jon Ross used should be examined.

Solution: The Resource Group blade is accessible.

Is the approach achieving the goal?

A. Yes

B. No

267. Your business's Azure membership includes a storage account, resource group, blob container, and file share.

Coworker Jon Ross installs a virtual machine and an extra Azure Storage account using a single Azure Resource Manager (ARM) template.

The ARM blueprint that Jon Ross used should be examined.

Solution: The Container blade is accessible.

Is the approach achieving the goal?

A. Yes

B. No

268. Three Virtual Machines (VMs) owned by your business are part of an availability group.

You attempt to resize one of the VMs, and an allocation failure notification is returned.

The VM must be resized immediately.

Which of the subsequent steps should you perform?

A. One of the VMs should be the only one you halt

B. Two of the VMs should be stopped

C. Disable all three virtual machines

D. You should take the required VM out of the availability group.

269. Your Azure Virtual Machine (VM) has a solitary data disc. You are responsible for connecting this data disc to another Azure virtual machine.

You must ensure that your plan enables virtual computers' shortest offline period.

What should you do first out of the options below?

A. End the virtual machine that houses the data disc

B. Disconnect the required data disc from the VM

C. Remove the hard drive

D. Remove the virtual machine that houses the data disc

270. Your business has an Azure subscription

Several Azure virtual machines (VMs) must be deployed using Azure Resource Manager (ARM) templates. The VMs will be a part of a particular availability set, as was told to you.

To ensure that as many VMs as possible can remain available during fabric failure or maintenance, you must ensure that the ARM template you set enables this.

Which of the following should you set as the platformFaultDomainCount property's value?

A. 10

B. 30

C. Min Value

D. Max Value

271. Your business has an Azure subscription.

Several Azure virtual machine (VMs) must be deployed using Azure Resource Manager (ARM) templates. The VMs will be a part of a particular Availability set, as was told to you.

To ensure that as many VMs as possible can remain available during fabric failure or maintenance, you must ensure that the ARM template you set enables this.

Which of the following should you set as the platformUpdateDomainCount property's value?

A. 10

B. 20

C. 30

D. 40

272. To coexist with the on-premises Active Directory domain in a hybrid fashion, your business has an Azure Active Directory (Azure AD) tenant.

Virtual Machines (VMs) operating on Windows Server 2012 R2 Hyper-V host servers make up the on-premise virtual environment.

You have developed some PowerShell scripts to automate the configuration of recently created VMs. You want to build several new virtual machines.

You require a system that guarantees the new VMs are used to execute the scripts.

Which of the following options is ideal?

A. Create a batch file called SetupComplete.cmd in the setup scripts subfolder under %windir%

B. Set up a Group Policy Object (GPO) to execute the programs during login

C. Set up a Group Policy Object (GPO) to use the starting scripts to execute the scripts

D. Create a new Virtual Hard Disc (VHD) and put the scripts on it.

273. To coexist with the on-premises Active Directory domain in a hybrid fashion, your business has an Azure Active Directory (Azure AD) tenant.

You will deploy several new virtual machines (VMs) in Azure. The operating system and specific software needs for the VMs will be the same.

In the on-premise virtual environment, you set up a reference virtual machine. The VM is then made more generic to produce a picture.

To ensure that the image is accessible for selection when you build new Azure VMs, you must upload it to Azure.

What PowerShell cmdlets should you employ?

A. Add-AzVM

B. Add-AzVhd

C. Add-AzImage

D. Add-AzImageDataDisk

274. Microsoft Azure hosts virtual machines (VMs) for your business. A single Azure virtual network called VNet1 contains all of the VMs.

Some users operate remotely for the company. The VMs on VNet1 must be accessible to remote employees.

It would help if you made access available to the remote employees.

What should you do?

A. Set up a Site-to-Site VPN (S2S)

B. Set up a VPN between VNets

C. Set up a P2S (Point-to-Site) VPN

D. Set up DirectAccess on a host VM running Windows Host 2012

E. Create a multi-site VPN

275. Your business owns two on-site computers called SRV01 and SR02. An application built by programmers utilizes SRV01. By IP address, the program invokes a service on SRV02.

You want to move the program to Virtual Machines (VMs) in Azure. On a single subnet in an Azure virtual network, you have set up two VMs.

The two virtual machines must be set up with static private IP addresses.

What should you do?

A. Execute the PowerShell commandlet New-AzureRMVMConfig

B. Execute the PowerShell commandlet Set-AzureSubnet

C. Make changes to the VM's settings in the Azure Management Portal

D. Make changes to Windows Network and Sharing Center's IP settings

E. Execute the PowerShell commandlet Set-AzureStaticVNetIP

276. Azure Active Directory (Azure AD) is a service your business subscribes to.

Five Virtual Machines (VMs) must be deployed to the virtual network subnet of your business.

Each VM will have a private and public IP address. The inbound and outbound security protocols must be identical for each virtual machine.

Which of the following configurations requires the fewest number of network interfaces?

A. 5

B. 10

C. 20

D. 40

277. Azure Active Directory (Azure AD) is a service your business subscribes to.

Five Virtual Machines (VMs) must be deployed to the virtual network subnet of your business.

Each VM will have a private and public IP address. The inbound and outbound security protocols must be identical for each virtual machine.

Which of the following configurations requires the fewest security groups?

A. 4

B. 3

C. 2

D. 1

278. Windows Server 2016-powered Azure virtual machines (VMs) are a part of your company's Azure subscription.

Every day, Azure Backup Instant Restore backs up one of the VMs.

You restore the VM's files when it is infected with data-encrypting ransomware.

Which statement about this situation is accurate?

A. Only the infected VM can be used to recover data

B. The data can be recovered to any VM the company's subscription covers

C. The files can only be recovered to a fresh VM

D. It won't be possible for you to retrieve the files

279. Windows Server 2016-powered Azure virtual machines (VMs) are a part of your company's Azure subscription.

Every day, Azure Backup Instant Restore backs up one of the VMs.

You need to restore the VM if it gets attacked with data-encrypting ransomware.

Which of the subsequent steps should you perform?

A. After erasing the infected VM, you should reinstall the original VM

B. You should restore the VM to any other VM included in the business contract

C. The VM should be restored to a fresh Azure VM

D. The VM should be restored to a Windows computer that is located on-site

280. You manage an Azure solution that is presently experiencing performance problems.

You must determine what is causing the metrics-related speed problems on the Azure infrastructure.

Which of the following should you employ as a tool?

A. Azure Traffic Analytics

B. Azure Monitor

C. Azure Activity Log

D. Azure Advisor

281. Your business has a Recovery Services vault as part of its Azure contract.

Your business's virtual machines (VMs) should be backed up to the Recovery Services vault using Azure Backup.

Which VMs from the list below can you back up? Decide which options apply.

A. Windows 10 virtual machines

B. Virtual machines running Windows Server 2012 or later

C. Virtual machines that are still running

D. Virtual machines with Debian 8.2+

E. Terminated virtual machines

282. You have a client called contoso.com in Azure Active Directory (Azure AD).

You have a CSV file with 500 external users' identities and email addresses.

Each of the 500 external users must have a guest user registration on contoso.com.

Solution: To run the New-AzureADUser cmdlet for each user, you build a PowerShell script.

Is the objective being met?

A. Yes

B. No

283. You have a client called contoso.com in Azure Active Directory (Azure AD).
You have a CSV file with 500 external users' identities and email addresses.
Each of the 500 external users must have a guest user registration on contoso.com.
Solution: Use the bulk create user action in Azure AD from the Azure portal.
Is the objective being met?

A. Yes

B. No

284. You have a client called contoso.com in Azure Active Directory (Azure AD).
You have a CSV file with 500 external users' identities and email addresses.
Each of the 500 external users must have a guest user registration on contoso.com.
Solution: You write a PowerShell routine that issues each external user a New-AzureADMSInvitation command.
Is the objective being met?

A. Yes

B. No

285. You have an Azure subscription with the Azure Kubernetes Service (AKS) cluster AKS1 and the user contoso.com from Azure Active Directory (Azure AD).
An administrator claims she cannot give customers of contoso.com access to AKS1.
You must make sure that users of contoso.com can gain entry to AKS1.
What should you start with?

A. Change the Organization relationships options on contoso.com

B. Create an OAuth 2.0 authentication endpoint from contoso.com

C. Produce AKS1

D. Create a category using AKS1

286. Your Azure Active Directory (Azure AD) and Microsoft 365 tenants are called contoso.com.

You want to give access to a temporary Microsoft SharePoint document library named Library1 to three users called User1, User2, and User3.

For individuals, groups must be created. The solution must ensure that after 180 days, the groups are deleted immediately.

Which two parties should your form? Each accurate response offers a complete resolution.

A. An organization using the Assigned membership type in Microsoft 365

B. An assigned membership type using a security group

C. A Microsoft 365 organization that makes use of the membership type Dynamic User

D. A Security group using the Dynamic User membership class

E. A Security group that makes use of the membership category for Dynamic Devices

287. You possess an Azure policy, as displayed in the illustration below:

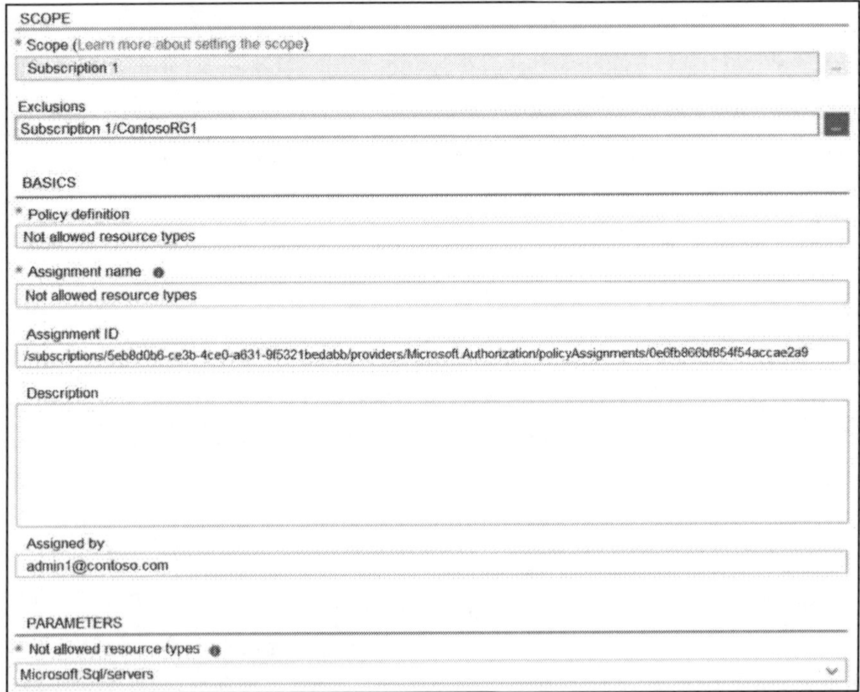

What impact does the strategy have?

A. Nowhere in Subscription 1 is it possible to create Azure SQL servers

B. Only in ContosoRG1 can Azure SQL servers be created

C. Only in ContosoRG1 are you unable to create Azure SQL Servers

D. Within Subscription 1, Azure SQL servers can be created in any resource category

288. You just made a new Azure subscription with a user called Admin1 in it. Admin1 tries to use an Azure Resource Manager template to install an Azure Marketplace resource. Admin1 uses Azure PowerShell to distribute the template and

encounters the following error: User failed resource buy validation. According to the error message, legal conditions have not been accepted for this item on this subscription. Please visit the Azure portal (http://go.microsoft.com/fwlink/?LinkId=534873) and setup programmatic deployment for the Marketplace item there or create it there for the first time if you have not already done so to approve the terms.

You must make sure that Admin1 can effectively deploy the Marketplace resource.

What should you do?

A. Run the Set-AzApiManagementSubscription command from Azure PowerShell

B. Sign up the Microsoft.Marketplace resource provider from the Azure interface

C. Use the Set-AzMarketplaceTerms command in Azure PowerShell

D. From the Azure portal, give Admin1 the position of billing administrator

289. There are 5,000 user profiles in your Azure Active Directory (Azure AD) tenant.

You make AdminUser1 a brand-new user.

It would help if you gave AdminUser1 the User administrator administrative position.

From the user account settings, what should you do?

A. Assign a new license using the Licenses blade

B. Change the directory job from the Directory role blade

C. Invite the user account to a new group using the Groups blade

290. There are 100 user profiles in your Azure Active Directory (Azure AD) tenant contoso.onmicrosoft.com.

For the renter, you buy 10 Azure AD Premium P2 licenses.

The Azure AD Premium capabilities must be accessible to 10 users.

What should you do?

A. From the Azure AD domain, add a business application

B. From each user's Groups blade, invite that user to a group

C. From the Azure AD Licenses blade, give a license

D. Change the directory position from each user's Directory role blade

291. You have a Microsoft System Center Service Manager on-premises implementation and Subscription1 Azure subscription.

There is a virtual machine called VM1 inside Subscription1.

You must create an alert in Service Manager when the memory on VM1 is less than 10%.

What should you start with?

A. Create an automation runbook

B. Deploy a function app

C. IT Service Management (ITSM) Connector deployment

D. Create a notification

292. You enroll in Azure Active Directory Premium P2 (Azure AD).

On every computer connected to the Azure AD domain, you must register a user with the email address admin1@contoso.com as an administrator.

What settings should you make in Azure AD?

A. The Devices blade's device configurations

B. The MFA Server blade's service providers

C. Settings from the Users tab for the user

D. Settings from the Groups blade, generally

293. You have a virtual network called VNet1 within your Azure subscription designated Subscription1. VNet1 belongs to the resource group RG1.

User1 is a subscriber of Subscription1. The following responsibilities apply to User1:

- Reader
- Security Admin
- Security Reader

You must ensure User1 can give other users the Reader function for VNet1.

What should you do?

A. Deactivate User1's Reader and Security responsibilities for Subscription1

B. Assign User1 the position of VNet1's User Access Administrator

C. Give VNet1's User1 the Network Contributor job

D. Give RG1's User1 the Network Contributor status

294. Azure Active Directory (Azure AD) tenancy contosocloud.onmicrosoft.com is what you have.

For contoso.com, your business has a public DNS zone.

You add contoso.com to Azure AD as a unique domain name.

Make sure Azure can validate the domain name.

Which kind of DNS entry should be set up?

A. MX

B. NSEC

C. PTR

D. RRSIG

295. Adatum is the name of your Azure Directory (Azure AD) tenancy, and Subscription1 is the name of your Azure Subscription. Developers is an organization that exists in Adatum.

There is a resource group called Dev in Subscription1.

The Developers group must have access to the Dev resource group's Azure logic app creation feature.

Solution: Give the Developers group on Subscription1 the DevTest Labs User status.

Is the objective being met?

A. Yes

B. No

296. Adatum is the name of your Azure Directory (Azure AD) tenancy, and Subscription1 is the name of your Azure Subscription. Developers is an organization that exists in Adatum.

There is a resource group called Dev in Subscription1.

The Developers group must have access to the Dev resource group's Azure logic app creation feature.

Solution: You give the Developers group the Logic App Operator job on Subscription1.

Is the objective being met?

A. Yes

B. No

297. Adatum is the name of your Azure Directory (Azure AD) tenancy, and Subscription1 is the name of your Azure Subscription. Developers is an organization that exists in Adatum.

There is a resource group called Dev in Subscription1.

The Developers group must have access to the Dev resource group's Azure logic app creation feature.

Solution: You give the Developers group the Contributor status on Dev.

Is the objective being met?

A. Yes

B. No

298. You have an Azure subscription called Subscription1 and a workplace in Azure Log Analytics.

You must use the table Event to examine the error events.

Which query should be executed in Workspace 1?

A. Get-Event Event | where "error" is equal to $_.EventType

B. Perform an event search for "error"

C. pick all events with EventType equal to "error"

D. Enter the command "search in (Event)* | where EventType equals 'error'" instead

299. You have a membership to Azure.

Users can use customers' sites or homes to obtain subscription tools. If users want to use Azure services from their residences, they must first set up a point-to-site VPN. Users on the client locations use site-to-site VPNs to access Azure services.

A line-of-business application you have called App1 is running on various Azure virtual machines. Windows Server 2016 is installed on virtual computers.

You must ensure that App1 is connected to every virtual computer.

Which two Azure applications are available for use? Each accurate response offers a complete resolution.

A. Internal load balancer

B. Public load balancer

C. Azure Content Delivery Network (CDN)

D. Traffic Manager

E. Azure Application Gateway

300. You have a membership to Azure.

There are 100 virtual computers in Azure.

It would help if you acted swiftly to locate idle virtual machines so that you can switch their service tier to a more affordable one.

Which blade should you employ?

A. Monitor

B. Advisor

C. Metrics

D. Customer insights

301. Azure Active Directory (Azure AD) tenancy contoso.onmicrosoft.com is what you have.

A user called Admin1 has been given the user administrator position.

A third party has a Microsoft account with the sign-in user1@outlook.com.

Unable to invite user user1@outlook.com "' Generic authorization exception,"' reads the error message when admin1 asks the external partner to join the Azure AD tenant.

It would help if you ensured that Admin1 has the authority to ask the outside party to log in to the Azure AD tenant.

What should you do?

A. Change the External cooperation options in the Users settings blade.

B. Add a unique domain from the unique domain names blade.

C. Add an identity supplier using the Organizational relationships blade.

D. Assign the Security administrator job to Admin1 using the Roles and administrators blade.

302. Your Azure Active Directory tenant is connected to your Azure account. A user account called User1 is part of the renter.

The tenant root administration group needs to be able to accept policies from User1, so make sure of this.

What should you do?

A. After giving User1 the Owner position for the Azure Subscription, change the pre-set conditional access policies

B. Give User1 the Owner position for the Azure subscription and tell them to set up access control for Azure resources

C. Give User1 the Global Administrator position and tell them to set up Azure resource access management

D. Establish a new management group and assign User1 the group administrator role

303. To activate Traffic Analytics for an Azure subscription, you must ensure that an Azure Active Directory (Azure AD) user named Admin1 has been given a crucial role.

Solution: You give Admin1 the Network Contributor position at the subscription level.

Is the objective being met?

A. Yes

B. No

304. To activate Traffic Analytics for an Azure subscription, you must ensure that an Azure Active Directory (Azure AD) user named Admin1 has been given a crucial role.

Solution: To Admin1, you grant the Owner position at the subscription level.

Is the objective being met?

A. Yes

B. No

305. To activate Traffic Analytics for an Azure subscription, you must ensure that an Azure Active Directory (Azure AD) user named Admin1 has been given a crucial role.

Solution: At the subscription level, Admin1 is given the Reader position.

Is the objective being met?

A. Yes

B. No

306. You have a user called User1 in your Azure subscription.

You must make sure User1 can handle virtual networks and deploy virtual machines. The least privilege concept must be applied to the solution.

Which position under Role-Based Access Control (RBAC) should be given to User1?

A. Owner

B. Virtual Machine Contributor

C. Contributor

D. Virtual Machine Administrator Login

307. You have a virtual machine called VM1 in Azure that is a part of your Subscription1 Azure subscription. A resource group called RG1 contains VM1.

Services that will be utilized to deploy resources to RG1 are operated by VM1.

You must ensure that an application using the identity of VM1 can control the resources in RG1 while it is running on VM1.

What should you start with?

A. Change VM1's Managed Identity options from the Azure portal

B. Change RG1's Access control (IAM) options from the Azure portal

C. Change VM1's Access control (IAM) options from the Azure portal

D. Change RG1's Policies options from the Azure portal

308. Adatum.com is the name of the Azure DNS zone you own.

A subdomain called research.adatum.com must be assigned to a separate DNS server in Azure.

What should you do?

A. In the adatum.com zone, create an NS record with the name study

B. In the adatum.com zone, create a PTR entry with the name research

C. Change adatum.com's SOA data

D. In the adatum.com zone, create an A record with the identifier *.research

309. You have an Azure subscription called Subscription1 and a workplace in Azure Log Analytics.

You must use the table Event to examine the error events.

Which query should be executed in Workspace 1?

A. Get-Event Event | where "error" is equal to $_.EventType

B. Event | search "error"

C. when EventType == "error," pick * from Event

D. where EventType is equal to "error," find in (Event) *

310. You have contoso.com listed as a DNS domain.

You establish the contoso.com public Azure DNS zone.

It would help if you ensured that any records generated in the contoso.com zone could be found online.

What should you do?

A. In contoso.com, create NS entries

B. Make changes to the DNS name registrar's SOA record

C. Set up a SOA entry on contoso.com

D. Make changes to the DNS name registrar's NS records

311. Your Azure Active Directory (Azure AD) entity already exists.

You intend to delete numerous users using the Azure Active Directory admin center's bulk delete feature.

For the bulk delete, you must make and upload a file.

What user characteristics should be present in the file?

A. Each user's utilization location and principal name only

B. Each user's sole primary user identity

C. Each user's unique display moniker only

D. Each user's display name and utilization location alone

E. Each user's primary user name and display name only

Answers

1. Answer: C

Explanation: First, we need to get the role definition.

```
$ipsrole = Get-AzRoleDefinition "Virtual Machine Contributor"
$ipsrole.Id = $null
$ipsrole.Name = "Virtual Machine Reader"
$ipsrole.Description = "Read permissions for virtual machines."
$ipsrole.Actions.Clear()
$ipsrole.Actions.Add("Microsoft.Storage/*/read")
$ipsrole.Actions.Add("Microsoft.Network/*/read")
$ipsrole.Actions.Add("Microsoft.Compute/*/read")
$ipsrole.AssignableScopes.Clear()
$ipsrole.AssignableScopes.Add("/subscriptions/00230400-0500-0440-0440-00555000000")
SLOT 2 -Role $ipsrole
```

All other options are incorrect.

For further details, you can visit the given URL.

https://docs.microsoft.com/en-us/azure/role-based-access-control/custom-roles-powershell

2. Answer: B

Explanation: The issue could be due to the security groups. You can diagnose the issue using IP Flow Verify.

Option A is incorrect since this is normally used from an application diagnostics perspective.

Option C is incorrect since this is used to provide recommendations on various types of Azure resources.

Option D is incorrect since this is used mainly from a security aspect in Azure.

For further details, you can visit the given URL.

https://docs.microsoft.com/en-us/azure/network-watcher/network-watcher-ip-flow-verify-overview

3. Answer: A, B, and E

Explanation: The Microsoft documentation lists steps for using the Azure File Sync service.

In this article

Prerequisites

Prepare Windows Server to use with Azure File Sync

Deploy the Storage Sync Service

Install the Azure File Sync agent (1)

Register Windows Server with Storage Sync Service (2)

Create a sync group and a cloud endpoint (3)

Create a server endpoint

Configure firewall and virtual network settings

Onboarding with Azure File Sync

Self-service restore through Previous Versions and VSS (Volume Shadow Copy Service)

Proactively recall new and changed files from an Azure file share

All other options are incorrect.

For further details, you can visit the given URL.

https://docs.microsoft.com/en-us/azure/storage/files/storage-sync-files-deployment-guide?tabs=portal

4. Answer: B

Explanation: The Export job feature only supports the BLOB service. This information is also available in the Microsoft documentation.

Supported storage types

The following list of storage types is supported with Azure Import/Export service.

Job	Storage Service	Supported	Not supported
Import	Azure Blob storage Azure File storage	Block Blobs and Page blobs supported Files supported	
Export	Azure Blob storage	Block blobs, Page blobs, and Append blobs supported	Azure Files not supported

Since this is mentioned, all other options are incorrect.

For further details, you can visit the given URL.

https://docs.microsoft.com/en-us/azure/storage/common/storage-import-export-requirements

5. Answer: B

Explanation: This can be done from the Firewall and virtual networks, as shown below.

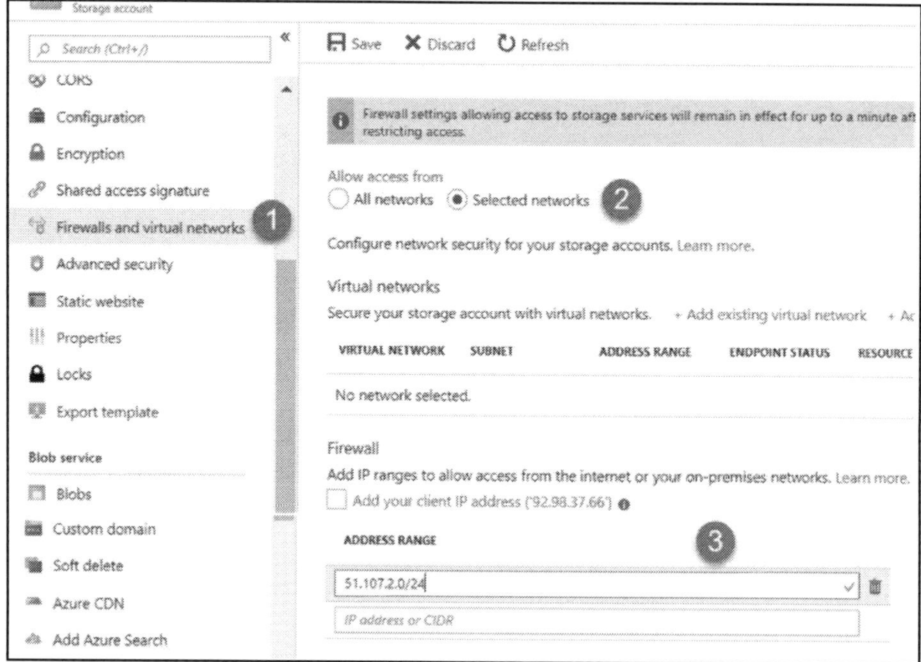

Ensure that "Selected networks" is selected before entering the IP address range. Since the explanation shows that all other options are invalid.

For further details, you can visit the given URL.

https://docs.microsoft.com/en-us/azure/storage/common/storage-network-security

6. Answer: C

Explanation: The issue is that no public IP address has been assigned to the Virtual Machine. This occurs as a result of the virtual machine being stopped. Therefore, you would need to start the Virtual machine. You will get a Public IP address and then connect to the Virtual Machine.

Network Interface: demovm1399 Effective security rules Topology
Virtual network/subnet: ipspecialist-rg/default Public IP: demovm1-ip Private IP: 10.0.0.5 Accelerated networking: Enabled

Inbound port rules Outbound port rules Application security groups Load balancing

Network security group demovm1-nsg (attached to network interface: demovm1399)
Impacts 0 subnets, 1 network interfaces

Add inbound port rule

PRIORITY	NAME	PORT	PROTOCOL	SOURCE	DESTINATION	ACTION	
100	Port_3389	3389	Any	Any	Any	Allow	...
65000	AllowVnetInBound	Any	Any	VirtualNetwork	VirtualNetwork	Allow	...
65001	AllowAzureLoadBalancerInBound	Any	Any	AzureLoadBalancer	Any	Allow	...
65500	DenyAllInBound	Any	Any	Any	Any	Deny	...

Option A is incorrect since this would stop the RDP connectivity.
Option B is incorrect since this is an Inbound connectivity issue.
Option C is incorrect since you cannot delete the default rules.

For further details, you can visit the given URL.

https://docs.microsoft.com/en-us/azure/virtual-network/virtual-network-ip-addresses-overview-arm

7. Answer: B

Explanation: Yes, this is one of the requirements.

For further details, you can visit the given URL.

https://docs.microsoft.com/en-us/azure/vpn-gateway/vpn-gateway-howto-point-to-site-resource-manager-portal

8. Answer: D

Explanation: An example of this is given in the Microsoft documentation.

Add the data disk to the virtual machine configuration with the Add-AzVMDataDisk command.

Azure PowerShell

```
$vm = Add-AzVMDataDisk `
    -VM $vm `
    -Name "myDataDisk" `
    -CreateOption Attach `
    -ManagedDiskId $dataDisk.Id `
    -Lun 1
```

Since this is given in the Microsoft documentation, all other options are incorrect.

For further details, you can visit the given URL.

https://docs.microsoft.com/en-us/azure/virtual-machines/windows/tutorial-manage-data-disk

9. Answer: A

Explanation: We would be able to move the resource **ipsnetwork** from the resource group **ips-rg1** to **ips-rg2**. The virtual network **ipsnetwork** has a Read-only lock. It means that we cannot delete or modify this resource without removing the lock. But this lock does not prevent us from moving a resource from one resource group to another. The current **ipsnetwork** resource group, **ips-rg1**, does not have any locks. The destination resource group, **ips-rg2**, has a Delete lock. This lock prevents the deletion of this resource group and all its resources. But it does not restrict the movement of the resources to this group from other groups.

For further details, you can visit the given URL.

https://docs.microsoft.com/en-us/azure/azure-resource-manager/management/lock-resources

10. Answer: C

Explanation: Access keys must be chosen in order to access the storage account since we must limit the use of secrets.

Option A is incorrect since this is used to enable or disable Cross-Origin Resource sharing.

Option C is incorrect since this is required to provide access to the storage account's resources for a specified period of time.

Option D is incorrect since we need to minimize the use of secrets. Hence, we cannot use the Managed Identity to access the Key vault to get the storage account keys' values.

For further details, you can visit the given URL.

https://docs.microsoft.com/en-us/azure/storage/common/storage-account-keys-manage

11. Answer: D

Explanation: For this requirement, the AKS clusters can use the Azure Container Networking Interface.

For further details, you can visit the given URL.

https://docs.microsoft.com/en-us/azure/aks/configure-kubenet

12. Answer: B

Explanation: To create a VNet-to-Vnet VPN between two virtual networks, you need to have a special subnet - gateway subnet. Azure recommends reserving/27 or /28 CIDR blocks for this subnet. The virtual network **vnet-staging-01** (10.10.10.0/24) has /24 CIDR blocks of address space. This space is already taken by the **vnet-staging-11** subnet (10.10.10.0/24). This is why there is no sufficient address space to create a gateway subnet and to establish a VNet-to-Vnet VPN connection between two VNETs. We need to resize the subnet space or create an additional IP address range for the gateway subnet.

For further details, you can visit the given URL.

https://docs.microsoft.com/en-us/azure/vpn-gateway/vpn-gateway-howto-vnet-vnet-resource-manager-portal

13, Answer: A

Explanation: The address spaces for the virtual networks do not overlap. You can establish a peering connection between both virtual networks.

For further details, you can visit the given URL.

https://docs.microsoft.com/en-us/azure/virtual-network/virtual-network-peering-overview

14. Answer: A

Explanation: In order to attach a network interface to a virtual machine, it must be created in the same region as the virtual machine. It also is a part of the same virtual network hosting the virtual machine.

For further details, you can visit the given URL.

https://docs.microsoft.com/en-us/azure/virtual-network/virtual-network-network-interface

15. Answer: D

Explanation: The network interface for a Virtual Machine can have both a private and public IP address.
So, by this measure, we only need to define 5 network interface cards, one for each virtual machine.
All the other options are incorrect.

For further details, you can visit the given URL.
https://docs.microsoft.com/en-us/azure/virtual-network/virtual-network-network-interface

16. Answer: B
Explanation: Standard_GRS, a geo-redundant storage, would ensure that data is available in a secondary region if the primary region goes down.
Options B and D are incorrect since these do not guarantee that data will be available if a region goes down.
Option C is incorrect since the costs would be more than Standard_GRS.

For further details, you can visit the given URL.
https://docs.microsoft.com/en-us/azure/storage/common/storage-redundancy-grs

17. Answer: C
Explanation: An example of this is given in the Microsoft documentation.

Update the virtual machine with the Update-AzVM command.

Azure PowerShell | Copy | Try It

```
Update-AzVM -ResourceGroupName "myResourceGroupDisk" -VM $vm
```

Since this is clearly given in the Microsoft documentation, all other options are incorrect.

For further details, you can visit the given URL.
https://docs.microsoft.com/en-us/azure/virtual-machines/windows/tutorial-manage-data-disk

18. Answer: A
Explanation: Yes, this is one of the requirements.
For more information on creating point-to-site VPN connections, please visit the below URL-

https://docs.microsoft.com/en-us/azure/vpn-gateway/vpn-gateway-howto-point-to-site-resource-manager-portal

19. Answer: B
Explanation: To access files from home computers, users have to use SMB protocol that expects port 445 to be open.

For further details, you can visit the given URL.
https://docs.microsoft.com/en-us/azure/storage/files/storage-how-to-use-files-windows

20. Answer: D
Explanation: To work with UNC path format, you have to mount the Azure file share with File Explorer. The UNC path format is as follows:

```
\\.file.core.windows.net
Or, in our case:
\\ipsstore.file.core.windows.net\demo
```

For further details, you can visit the given URL.
https://docs.microsoft.com/en-us/azure/storage/files/storage-how-to-use-files-windows

21. Answer: B
Explanation: To work with UNC path format, you have to mount the Azure file share with File Explorer. The UNC path format is as follows:

```
\\.file.core.windows.net
Or, in our case:
\\ipsstore.file.core.windows.net\demo
```

For further details, you can visit the given URL.
https://docs.microsoft.com/en-us/azure/storage/files/storage-how-to-use-files-windows

22. Answer: C
Explanation: To work with UNC path format, you have to mount the Azure file share with File Explorer. The UNC path format is as follows:

```
\\.file.core.windows.net
Or, in our case:
\\ipsstore.file.core.windows.net\demo
```

For further details, you can visit the given URL.
https://docs.microsoft.com/en-us/azure/storage/files/storage-how-to-use-files-windows

23. Answer: C

Explanation: If RuleB is deleted, users will not be able to access port 80 and the web server.

There is a Deny rule of RuleA for ports 50-60. Since DNS listens on port 53, you will not be able to access the DNS server. But you will still be able to connect to the virtual machine using RDP under the Allow_rdp rule.

Because of this logic, all other options are incorrect.

For further details, you can visit the given URL.
https://docs.microsoft.com/en-us/azure/virtual-network/security-overview

24. Answer: B

Explanation: This can be done from the Firewall and virtual networks, as shown below.

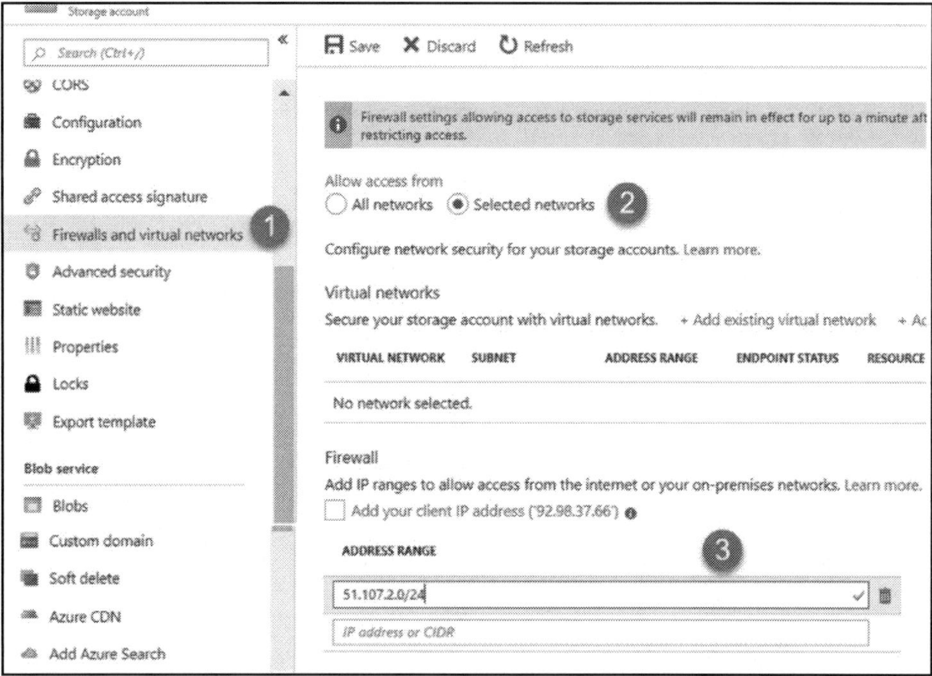

Ensure to click on "Selected networks" and then enter the IP address range. Since the explanation shows that all other options are invalid.

For further details, you can visit the given URL.

https://docs.microsoft.com/en-us/azure/storage/common/storage-network-security

25. Answer: D

Explanation: This can be done from the Soft delete section for the BLOB service, as shown below.

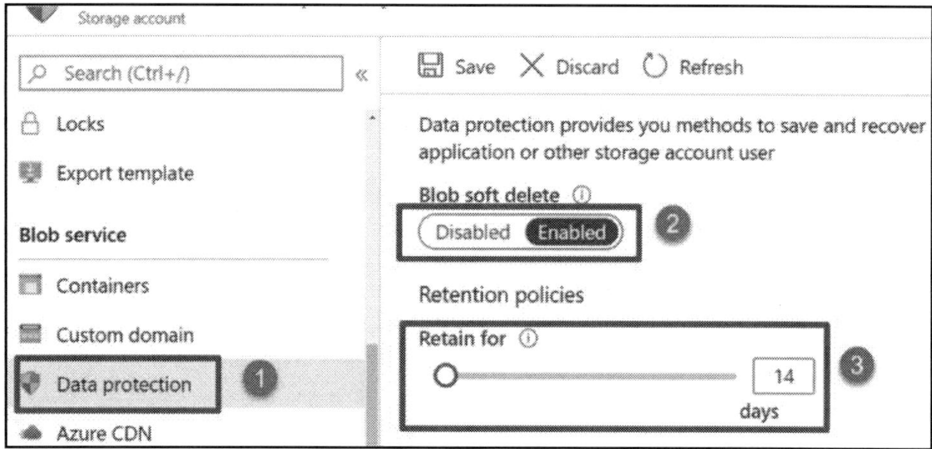

Since the explanation shows that all other options are invalid.

For further details, you can visit the given URLs.

https://docs.microsoft.com/en-us/azure/storage/blobs/soft-delete-blob-overview

https://docs.microsoft.com/en-us/azure/storage/blobs/soft-delete-blob-enable?tabs=azure-portal

26. Answer: A

Explanation: SLOT 1 covers the word "deployment".

```
az group create --name  ips-rg   --location "Central US"
az deployment group create \
  --name  ipsdeployment  \
  --resource-group   ips-rg   \
  --template-file storage.json \
```

All other options are incorrect.

For further details, you can visit the given URL.

https://docs.microsoft.com/en-us/azure/azure-resource-manager/resource-group-template-deploy-cli

27. Answer: B

Explanation: SLOT 2 covers the "--template-file" option.

```
az group create --name  ips-rg  --location "Central US"
az deployment group create \
  --name  ipsdeployment  \
  --resource-group  ips-rg  \
  --template-file storage.json \
```

All other options are incorrect.
For further details, you can visit the given URL.
https://docs.microsoft.com/en-us/azure/azure-resource-manager/resource-group-template-deploy-cli

28. Answer: B
Explanation: Role-based access control can be used to restrict access to resources. But RBAC does not put any governance on what type of resources to create. If you need to limit resource creation, like provision VM only of a particular SKU, you need to implement Azure policies.
For further details, you can visit the given URL.
https://docs.microsoft.com/en-us/azure/role-based-access-control/overview

29. Answer: B
Explanation: Azure locks are used to prevent users from accidentally deleting or modifying critical resources. If you need to limit the resource creation, like provision VM only of a particular SKU, you need to implement Azure policies.
For further details, you can visit the given URL.
https://docs.microsoft.com/en-us/azure/azure-resource-manager/resource-group-lock-resources

30. Answer: A
Explanation: Yes, this can be done with Azure policies. There is also already an in-built policy that can implement this policy, as shown below.

Allowed virtual machine SKUs
Policy definition

Assign | Edit definition | Duplicate definition | Delete definition

Name : Allowed virtual machine SKUs
Description : This policy enables you to specify a set of virtual machine SKUs that your organization can d...
Effect : Deny
Category : Compute

Definition location : --
Definition ID : /providers/Microsoft.Authorization/
Type : Built-in
Mode : Indexed

Definition | Assignments (0) | Parameters

```
{
  "properties": {
    "displayName": "Allowed virtual machine SKUs",
    "policyType": "BuiltIn",
    "mode": "Indexed",
    "description": "This policy enables you to specify a set of virtual machine SKUs that your organization can deploy.",
    "metadata": {
      "category": "Compute"
    },
```

For further details, you can visit the given URL.
https://docs.microsoft.com/en-us/azure/governance/policy/samples/allowed-skus-storage

31. Answer: D

Explanation: This can be done with the IP Flow Verify feature.

Option A is incorrect since this feature is used to get the next hop type and IP address of a specific VM packet.

Option B is incorrect since this feature is used for deep-dive network packet capture.

Option C is incorrect since this feature is a cloud-based solution that provides visibility into user and application activity in cloud networks.

For further details, you can visit the given URL.
https://docs.microsoft.com/en-us/azure/network-watcher/network-watcher-ip-flow-verify-overview

32. Answer: B

Explanation: Azure locks are used to prevent users from accidentally deleting or modifying critical resources. If you need to limit the resource creation, like provision VM only of a particular SKU, you need to implement Azure policies.

For further details, you can visit the given URL.
https://docs.microsoft.com/en-us/azure/azure-resource-manager/resource-group-lock-resources

33. Answer: B

Explanation: This can be done with the Connection Monitor feature. The Microsoft documentation mentions the following.

The connection Monitor monitors communication at regular intervals. It informs you of changes in reachability and latency. You can also check the current and historical network topology between source agents and destination endpoints. Sources can be Azure VMs or on-premises machines with an installed monitoring agent.

For further details, you can visit the given URL.

https://docs.microsoft.com/en-us/azure/network-watcher/connection-monitor-overview

34. Answer: C

Explanation: You can achieve 99.99% SLA on your virtual machines' infrastructure level by deploying them across availability zones.

For further details, you can visit the given URL.

https://docs.microsoft.com/en-us/azure/availability-zones/az-overview

35. Answer: D

Explanation: The task requires supporting the Hot, Cool, and Archive tiers. There is only one option from our list of options that can provide this: StorageV2 or General Purpose v2 Storage Account. With this storage account type, we will have the complete functionality of the BLOB service.

For further details, you can visit the given URL.

https://docs.microsoft.com/en-us/azure/storage/common/storage-account-overview

36. Answer: C

Explanation: The query will return events for the last 14 days.

We are using Kusto Query Language (KQL) for this query. The query needs to calculate the time between startofweek(ago(9d)) and endofweek(ago(2d))

In KQL start of the week usually is **Sunday**. If today is Monday, the 21st, 9 days ago was Saturday, the 12th. But we are looking for the start of the week for this Saturday, the 12th. It was Sunday, the 6th.

Our startofweek(ago(9d)) is Sunday, the 6th.

In KQL end of the week usually is **Saturday**. If today is Monday, the 21st, 2 days ago was Saturday, the 19th. This is precisely the end of the previous week.

Our endofweek(ago(2d)) is Saturday, the 19th.

The difference between endofweek(ago(2d))-startofweek(ago(9d)) is 2 full weeks or 14 days.

A week number one - from Sunday, 6th, till Saturday, 12th - 7 days.

A week number two - from Sunday, 13th, till Saturday, 19th, - 7 days

For further details, you can visit the given URLs.
https://docs.microsoft.com/en-us/azure/azure-monitor/log-query/log-query-overview
https://docs.microsoft.com/en-us/azure/data-explorer/kusto/query/
https://docs.microsoft.com/en-us/azure/data-explorer/kusto/query/startofweekfunction
https://docs.microsoft.com/en-us/azure/data-explorer/kusto/query/endofweekfunction

37. Answer: B

Explanation: If you try to run the query in Log Analytics, you will see the below output. It consists of a graph that has the Average of the Counter value on the Y-axis.
Since the explanation shows that all other options are invalid.
For further details, you can visit the given URL.
https://docs.microsoft.com/en-us/azure/azure-monitor/log-query/log-query-overview

38. Answer: B, D, and E

Explanation: If the VPN device that you want to connect to has changed its public IP address, you need to modify the local network gateway to reflect that change. If a gateway connection already exists, you first need to remove the connection. After removing the connection, you can modify the gateway IP address and recreate a new connection. You can also modify the address prefixes at the same time. This results in some downtime for your VPN connection. When modifying the gateway IP address, you do not need to delete the VPN gateway. You only need to remove the connection.
Since this is clearly mentioned in the Microsoft documentation, all other options are incorrect.
For further details, you can visit the given URL.
https://docs.microsoft.com/en-us/azure/vpn-gateway/vpn-gateway-create-site-to-site-rm-powershell

39. Answer: A and C

Explanation: Since we need to distribute traffic across the virtual machines, we can use either the Load Balancer or Application Gateway service.
The other options are incorrect since the users access the Azure virtual machines via private IP addresses. This is because the users are connecting via VPNs. Therefore, we need to use internal load-balancing solutions.

For further details, you can visit the given URLs.
https://docs.microsoft.com/en-us/azure/load-balancer/load-balancer-overview
https://docs.microsoft.com/en-us/azure/application-gateway/overview

40. Answer: D
Explanation: This can be accomplished by the Storage Account Contributor.
For further details, you can visit the given URL.
https://docs.microsoft.com/en-us/azure/role-based-access-control/built-in-roles

41. **Answer: C**
Explanation: This can be accomplished with the Storage Blob Data Contributor.
For further details, you can visit the given URL.
https://docs.microsoft.com/en-us/azure/role-based-access-control/built-in-roles

42. Answer: B
Explanation: This can be accomplished by the Storage Blob Data Owner.
For further details, you can visit the given URL.
https://docs.microsoft.com/en-us/azure/role-based-access-control/built-in-roles

43. Answer: B
Explanation: Only the Blob service is supported by the Export job feature.
For further details, you can visit the given URL.
https://docs.microsoft.com/en-us/azure/storage/common/storage-import-export-requirements

44. Answer: C
Explanation: An example of this is given in the Microsoft documentation.
Create the initial configuration with New-AzDiskConfig. The following example configures a disk that is 128 gigabytes in size.

Azure PowerShell

```
$diskConfig = New-AzDiskConfig `
   -Location "EastUS" `
   -CreateOption Empty `
   -DiskSizeGB 128
```

For further details, you can visit the given URL.
https://docs.microsoft.com/en-us/azure/virtual-machines/windows/tutorial-manage-data-disk

45. Answer: A

Explanation: An example of this is given in the Microsoft documentation.
Create the data disk with the New-AzDisk command.

Azure PowerShell

```
$dataDisk = New-AzDisk `
  -ResourceGroupName "myResourceGroupDisk" `
  -DiskName "myDataDisk" `
  -Disk $diskConfig
```

For further details, you can visit the given URL.
https://docs.microsoft.com/en-us/azure/virtual-machines/windows/tutorial-manage-data-disk

46. Answer: B

Explanation: An example of this is given in the Microsoft documentation.
Get the virtual machine that you want to add the data disk to with the Get-AzVM command.

Azure PowerShell

```
$vm = Get-AzVM -ResourceGroupName "myResourceGroupDisk" -Name "myVM"
```

For further details, you can visit the given URL.
https://docs.microsoft.com/en-us/azure/virtual-machines/windows/tutorial-manage-data-disk

47. Answer: D

Explanation: An example of this is given in the Microsoft documentation.
Add the data disk to the virtual machine configuration with the Add-AzVMDataDisk command.

Azure PowerShell

```
$vm = Add-AzVMDataDisk `
  -VM $vm `
  -Name "myDataDisk" `
  -CreateOption Attach `
  -ManagedDiskId $dataDisk.Id `
  -Lun 1
```

For further details, you can visit the given URL.
https://docs.microsoft.com/en-us/azure/virtual-machines/windows/tutorial-manage-data-disk

48. Answer: C

Explanation: To replace the virtual machine's existing disks, it must be in the Stopped or Deallocated state.
For further details, you can visit the given URL.
https://docs.microsoft.com/en-us/azure/backup/backup-azure-arm-restore-vms#replace-existing-disks

49. Answer: B

Explanation: Since the policy is applied to the Tenant Root Group, it would be applied to all subscriptions and resource groups. If you need to create a virtual machine, you must have permission to create virtual network resources required for VM provisioning. Hence, the policy restricts the creation of VNet resources. You would not be able to create a new VM in this resource group.
For further details, you can visit the given URL.
https://docs.microsoft.com/en-us/azure/governance/policy/overview

50. Answer: A

Explanation: To ensure that traffic can be forwarded across networks, you need to enable forwarded traffic settings.
This is like the Hub and spoke model given in the Microsoft documentation wherein you need to enable forwarded traffic.
For further details, you can visit the given URL.
https://docs.microsoft.com/en-us/azure/architecture/reference-architectures/hybrid-networking/hub-spoke

51. Answer: B

Explanation: In order to ensure that traffic is routed via the intrusion-based device, you need to set up a routing table and add the routing table to the subnets in the other virtual networks.
For further details, you can visit the given URL.
https://docs.microsoft.com/en-us/azure/virtual-network/tutorial-create-route-table-portal
https://docs.microsoft.com/en-us/azure/virtual-wan/scenario-route-through-nva

52. Answer: C

Explanation: In order to ensure traffic can be forwarded, you need to enable IP forwarding.

This is clearly mentioned in the Microsoft documentation; all other options are incorrect.

For further details, you can visit the given URL.

https://docs.microsoft.com/en-us/azure/virtual-network/tutorial-create-route-table-portal

53. Answer: B

Explanation: Azure policies are used from a governance perspective and cannot be used to create bills department-wise.

For further details, you can visit the given URL.

https://docs.microsoft.com/en-us/azure/governance/policy/overview

54. Answer: A

Explanation: Yes, you can use resource tags to organize your Azure resources and also apply billing techniques department-wise.

For further details, you can visit the given URL.

https://docs.microsoft.com/en-us/azure/azure-resource-manager/management/tag-resources

55. Answer: B

Explanation: This is used to control access to resources and cannot be used for billing purposes.

For further details, you can visit the given URL.

https://docs.microsoft.com/en-us/azure/role-based-access-control/overview

56. Answer: A

Explanation: The Not allowed resource types policy is only applied to the resource group **ips-rg**. You can move the virtual machine to another resource group.

For further details, you can visit the given URL.

https://docs.microsoft.com/en-us/azure/governance/policy/overview

57. Answer: B

Explanation: Azure policies would only highlight the compliance of existing resources and enforce the policy restrictions on new resources. As a result, the virtual machine's state would not change.

For further details, you can visit the given URL.

https://docs.microsoft.com/en-us/azure/governance/policy/overview

58. Answer: B
Explanation: You are unable to alter the virtual networks because of a policy that prohibits any actions on virtual networks.
For further details, you can visit the given URL.
https://docs.microsoft.com/en-us/azure/governance/policy/overview

59. Answer: C
Explanation: The format of the prefixMatch is container/folder: **demo/data**
For further details, you can visit the given URL.
https://docs.microsoft.com/en-us/azure/storage/blobs/storage-lifecycle-management-concepts

60. Answer: B
Explanation: Since the question states that we need to move the objects to the cool tier after 30 days, this should be the value for tierToCool.
For further details, you can visit the given URL.
https://docs.microsoft.com/en-us/azure/storage/blobs/storage-lifecycle-management-concepts

61. Answer: C
Explanation: Since the question states that we need to move the objects to the archive tier after 90 days, this should be the value for tierToArchive.
For further details, you can visit the given URL.
https://docs.microsoft.com/en-us/azure/storage/blobs/storage-lifecycle-management-concepts

62. Answer: D
Explanation: The URL for accessing an object must be https://< storageAccountName>.blob.core.windows.net / <containerName>/<objectName>: https://ipspecialiststore.blob.core.windows.net/demo/audio.log
For further details, you can visit the given URL.
https://docs.microsoft.com/en-us/azure/storage/blobs/storage-blobs-introduction

63. Answer: A
Explanation: The secure way to implement this is to generate a shared access signature.
All of the other ways are incorrect since they do not provide secure access to the storage account object.

For further details, you can visit the given URL.
https://docs.microsoft.com/en-us/azure/storage/common/storage-sas-overview

64. Answer: A

Explanation: The Activity Log service provides insights for all resource activities within your subscription.

You can create alerts based on the Activity logs.

For further details, you can visit the given URL.
https://docs.microsoft.com/en-us/azure/azure-monitor/platform/activity-log

65. Answer: B

Explanation: The Azure Advisor service is used as a recommendation engine and cannot be used to record virtual machines' activities.

For further details, you can visit the given URL.
https://docs.microsoft.com/en-us/azure/advisor/advisor-overview

66. Answer: B

Explanation: The Service Health service is used to inform users of the health of Azure-based services.

For further details, you can visit the given URL.
https://azure.microsoft.com/en-us/features/service-health

67. Answer: C

Explanation: We need to keep costs minimized. There is no mention in the question on Fault tolerance and disaster recovery. We can opt for Local Redundant storage.

Since this is the most cost-effective approach, all other options are incorrect.

For further details, you can visit the given URL.
https://docs.microsoft.com/en-us/azure/storage/common/storage-redundancy

68. Answer: A

Explanation: For the Virtual network, you need to have a gateway subnet.

The virtual network gateway uses a specific subnet called the gateway subnet. The gateway subnet is part of the virtual network IP address range that you specify when configuring your virtual network. It contains the IP addresses that the virtual network gateway resources and services use.

Since this is clearly mentioned in the documentation, all other options are incorrect.

For further details, you can visit the given URL.

https://docs.microsoft.com/en-us/azure/vpn-gateway/vpn-gateway-howto-site-to-site-resource-manager-portal

69. Answer: A

Explanation: You need to add an inbound security rule and not an Outbound Security rule.

For further details, you can visit the given URL.

https://docs.microsoft.com/en-us/azure/virtual-network/security-overview

70. Answer: A

Explanation: We would be able to move the resource **ipsstore2090** from the resource group **ips-rg1** to **ips-rg2.** The storage account **ipsstore2090** has a Delete lock. It means that we cannot delete this resource without removing the lock. But this lock does not prevent us from moving a resource from one resource group to another. The current **ipsstore2090** resource group, **ips-rg1**, does not have any locks. The destination resource group **ips-rg2,** similar to the storage account, has a Delete lock. This lock prevents the deletion of this resource group and all its resources. But it does not restrict the movement of the resources to this group from other groups.

For further details, you can visit the given URL.

https://docs.microsoft.com/en-us/azure/azure-resource-manager/management/lock-resources

71. Answer: A

Explanation: We would be able to move the resource **ipsip** from the resource group **ips-rg1** to **ips-rg2.** The public IP address **ipsip** and it is resource group **ips-rg1** do not have any locks. The destination resource group, **ips-rg2**, has a Delete lock. This lock prevents the deletion of this resource group and all resources within it. But it does not restrict the movement of the resources to this group from other groups.

For more information on resource locks, please visit the following URL-

https://docs.microsoft.com/en-us/azure/azure-resource-manager/management/lock-resources

72. Answer: A

Explanation: ipsusr1 user has the Global Administrator role and has created the new directory. The user would have the required permissions to create new users in the directory.

For further details, you can visit the given URL.

https://docs.microsoft.com/en-us/azure/active-directory/fundamentals/active-directory-access-create-new-tenant

73. Answer: B

Explanation: The user **ipsusr2** is only the Global Administrator for the ipspecialist.onmicrosoft.com directory. To add users to the new **staging.ipspecialist.onmicrosoft.com** directory, **ipsusr2** needs to have the required role in the new directory.

For further details, you can visit the given URL.

https://docs.microsoft.com/en-us/azure/active-directory/fundamentals/active-directory-access-create-new-tenant

74. Answer: B

Explanation: The user **ipsusr3** is only the User Administrator for the ipspecialist.onmicrosoft.com directory. To add users to the new **staging.ipspecialist.onmicrosoft.com** directory, **ipsusr3** needs to have the required role in the new directory.

For further details, you can visit the given URL.

https://docs.microsoft.com/en-us/azure/active-directory/fundamentals/active-directory-access-create-new-tenant

75. Answer: B

Explanation: To create a VNet-to-Vnet VPN between two virtual networks, you need to have a special subnet - gateway subnet. Azure recommends reserving/27 or /28 CIDR blocks for this subnet. The virtual network **vnet-staging-01** (10.10.10.0/24) has /24 CIDR blocks of address space. This space is already taken by the **vnet-staging-11** subnet (10.10.10.0/24). This is why there is no sufficient address space to create a gateway subnet and to establish a VNet-to-Vnet VPN connection between two VNETs. We need to resize the subnet space or create an additional IP address range for the gateway subnet.

For further details, you can visit the given URL.

https://docs.microsoft.com/en-us/azure/vpn-gateway/vpn-gateway-howto-vnet-vnet-resource-manager-portal

76. Answer: A

Explanation: The address spaces for the virtual networks do not overlap. You can establish a peering connection between both virtual networks.

For further details, you can visit the given URL.

https://docs.microsoft.com/en-us/azure/virtual-network/virtual-network-peering-overview

77. Answer: B
Explanation: If you look at an example of the default network security rules, only traffic inbound within the virtual network and traffic from the load balancer is allowed. Otherwise, all other traffic is denied. Hence, here also, the traffic will be denied.

For further details, you can visit the given URL.
https://docs.microsoft.com/en-us/azure/virtual-network/security-overview

78. Answer: A
Explanation: Since there is a rule that allows remote desktop connections from any source, connections are possible into **vmips2.**

For further details, you can visit the given URL.
https://docs.microsoft.com/en-us/azure/virtual-network/security-overview

79. Answer: B
Explanation: If we would not add **nsg-ips1** to **SubnetA**, then RDP to **vmips1** is **possible**. Since we have created a Windows VM, the RDP port is, by default, added to Inbound rules.

- In the given scenario, we are creating a new NSG called nsg-ips1, and it does not have an **RDP** port added to it.

We need to get it added by creating a new rule.

- **Due to this reason, "remote desktop" to vmips2 from vmips1 is not possible**

For further details, you can visit the given URL.
https://docs.microsoft.com/en-us/azure/virtual-network/security-overview

80. Answer: C
Explanation: The Recovery Services vault and the virtual machine needs to be in the same region. This condition is fulfilled by the **vmips1, vmips3, vmipsA, and vmipsC** virtual machines.

Because of the satisfaction of this condition, all other options are incorrect.

For further details, you can visit the given URL.
https://docs.microsoft.com/en-us/azure/backup/backup-azure-vms-first-look-arm

81. Answer: A

Explanation: The network interface needs to be created in the same region as the virtual network.

For further details, you can visit the given URL.

https://docs.microsoft.com/en-us/azure/virtual-network/virtual-network-network-interface

82. Answer: A

Explanation: The Azure Import/Export service supports only data export from Azure Blob storage.

For further details, you can visit the given URL.

https://docs.microsoft.com/en-us/azure/storage/common/storage-import-export-service

83. Answer: B

Explanation: In this task, there are three types of resources that require a backup. One of them is the Azure SQL database. We do not need to create a daily backup for Azure SQL Database because Azure provides a backup as an automatic service for every database by default. Azure SQL Database is an Azure fully managed platform-as-a-service (PaaS) database engine. It includes automatic patching, monitoring, and backups. Azure SQL Database service is different from SQL Server that runs in Azure VM. SQL Server in VM requires the user to provide database maintenance and set up backups.

For two other types, Azure VM and Azure File shares, we need to create daily backup policies. For multiple VMs, Microsoft recommends creating a Recovery Services vault and adding backup policies from the Backup Policies option.

For further details, you can visit the given URL.

https://docs.microsoft.com/en-us/azure/backup/backup-azure-vms-first-look-arm

84. Answer: C

Explanation: The storage account must be in the same region as the Recovery Services vault to store the reports. This is why **storeips2090** is the correct answer. All other options are incorrect.

For further details, you can visit the given URL.

https://docs.microsoft.com/en-us/azure/backup/configure-reports

85. Answer: D

Explanation: The Log Analytics workspace can be in any region. It does not need to be in the same region as the recovery services vault.

For further details, you can visit the given URL.

https://docs.microsoft.com/en-us/azure/backup/configure-reports

86. Answer: B

Explanation: Once you add a cloud endpoint to a Sync group, you cannot add any other shares as the cloud endpoint.

For further details, you can visit the given URL.

https://docs.microsoft.com/en-us/azure/storage/files/storage-sync-files-deployment-guide?tabs=azure-portal

87. Answer: A

Explanation: As **ipsshare2** has not been added as a server endpoint, you can add it as the server endpoint.

For further details, you can visit the given URL.

https://docs.microsoft.com/en-us/azure/storage/files/storage-sync-files-deployment-guide?tabs=azure-portal

88. Answer: B

Explanation: We can have more than 1 server endpoint if the namespaces of these endpoints are not overlapping and are on the same volume. In this problem, the folders are on different drives, and hence it is not possible.

For further details, you can visit the given URL.

https://docs.microsoft.com/en-us/azure/storage/files/storage-sync-files-server-endpoint

89. Answer: A

Explanation: When configuring MFA to a user, we must provide valid options to validate the action.

In the given table, **ipsusr2** does not have a valid mode of getting an MFA request approved, i.e., neither Office Phone / Mobile Number is provided for validation. This makes it possible to validate the MFA request by providing a mobile phone number. In the given table, **ipsusr4** already has an Office Phone assigned, and that is enough for validating MFA in case the user is working from Office. If the user is working remotely, then MFA validation fails, and for that, adding a Mobile Phone Number will allow the login to be successful.

Due to these reasons, the answer is **Yes**

For further details, you can visit the given URL.
https://docs.microsoft.com/en-us/azure/active-directory/authentication/concept-mfa-howitworks

90. Answer: A

Explanation: The premise given here is for all the users, and this question is asking if "**adding**" of "**office phone number**" to **ipsusr2** will allow **MFA** assigned?
And this is possible because to configure MFA, we need to have a valid contact number, and in this case, we are adding an "office phone number". The authentication call will be coming to the given phone number before authorizing the user.

For further details, you can visit the given URL.
https://docs.microsoft.com/en-us/azure/active-directory/user-help/multi-factor-authentication-setup-office-phone

91. Answer: A

Explanation: Yes, since MFA cannot be enabled for external user accounts. Even if MFA is enabled for all users, it is not enabled for external accounts. User **ipsusr3** has typed "Guest" in Azure AD. To force **ipsusr3** to use MFA, we have to create a new user account for him in Azure AD.
If we implement the Conditional Access option, we would not be required to add this user to Azure AD. Conditional Access will force ipsusr3 to use MFA.

For further details, you can visit the given URL.
https://docs.microsoft.com/en-us/azure/active-directory/authentication/concept-mfa-howitworks

92. Answer: A

Explanation: The Microsoft documentation clearly states that the replication type of the storage account can be changed to Zone redundant storage only if the current replication technique is either LRS or GRS.

For further details, you can visit the given URL.
https://docs.microsoft.com/en-us/azure/storage/common/redundancy-migration?tabs=portal

93. Answer: B

Explanation: For this requirement, the AKS clusters can use.

For further details, you can visit the given URL.
https://docs.microsoft.com/en-us/azure/aks/configure-kubenet

94. Answer: C

Explanation: If we need to deploy **ipsapp1** in the East US region, we must choose the App Service Plan in the same region. The Web App and the App Service Plan need to be located in the same region.

There are two plans in the East US region: **ipsplanA** and **ipsplanB**. You can deploy a .Net Core application on either a Windows OS or a Linux OS.
For further details, you can visit the given URLs.
https://docs.microsoft.com/en-us/azure/app-service/overview-hosting-plans
https://docs.microsoft.com/en-us/azure/app-service/app-service-plan-manage

95. Answer: B

Explanation: An ASP.NET v4.7 application cannot be deployed to Linux in Azure. Below is the screenshot from the Create Web App screen in Azure Portal.

As you can see Linux option is disabled.
Other options are incorrect.

For further details, you can visit the given URL.
https://docs.microsoft.com/en-us/azure/app-service/overview

96. Answer: C

Explanation: To deploy an application to the cluster, you have to use a Kubernetes manifest file. This YAML file contains information about which ACR image to run. Then you can use kubectl to apply the command to deploy the application to the cluster.

All other options are incorrect.

For further details, you can visit the given URL.
https://docs.microsoft.com/en-us/azure/aks/kubernetes-walkthrough

97. Answer: B

Explanation: To work with Log Analytics data, use the Kusto Query language (KQL).

For further details, you can visit the given URLs.
https://docs.microsoft.com/en-us/azure/azure-monitor/log-query/get-started-queries
https://docs.microsoft.com/en-us/learn/modules/analyze-infrastructure-with-azure-monitor-logs/3-create-log-queries

98. Answer: A

Explanation: This resource can be added to the resource group because it is an isolated resource.

For further details, you can visit the given URL.
https://docs.microsoft.com/en-us/azure/azure-resource-manager/management/move-resource-group-and-subscription

99. Answer: A

Explanation: The network interface can be moved to another resource group, even if it is a part of an existing virtual network. We do not need to move the associated resources of the network interface along with it. It is "**optional,**" i.e.; we can ignore the moving of resources.

For further details, you can visit the given URL.
https://docs.microsoft.com/en-us/azure/azure-resource-manager/management/move-resource-group-and-subscription

100. Answer: B

Explanation: The location of the resource would remain as it is. It is only the resource group that changes.

For further details, you can visit the given URL.

https://docs.microsoft.com/en-us/azure/azure-resource-manager/management/move-resource-group-and-subscription

101. Answer: C

Explanation: The maximum possible number of fault domains in an availability set is 3. Since we must ensure that the maximum possible number of virtual machines are available when the fabric fails, we must choose the value of 3.

For further details, you can visit the given URL.

https://docs.microsoft.com/en-us/azure/virtual-machines/windows/manage-availability

102. Answer: D

Explanation: First, we have to ensure that the maximum possible number of virtual machines are available when the fabric fails. We need to choose the value of 20. The maximum number of fault domains possible in an availability set is 3.

For further details, you can visit the given URL.

https://docs.microsoft.com/en-us/azure/virtual-machines/windows/manage-availability

103. Answer: B

Explanation: Here, we need to provide time-bound access. We need to make use of Shared Access Signatures.

Option A is incorrect since this is used to enable or disable Cross-Origin Resource sharing.

Option C is incorrect since this does not provide time-bound access.

Option D is incorrect since we need to minimize the use of secrets. Hence, we cannot use the Managed Identity to access the Key vault to get the storage account keys' values.

For further details, you can visit the given URL.

https://docs.microsoft.com/en-us/azure/storage/common/storage-sas-overview

104. Answer: B

Explanation: Availability sets cannot protect virtual machines from a data center-level failure. Availability zones protect VMs from data center failure.

You need to distribute your virtual machines across three availability zones. Microsoft provides this in the following documentation.

At the table below we can see the two main differences between Availability Set, Zone

Availability Set	Availability Zone
Protect from Hardware failures within data centers	Protect from entire data center failure
SLA 99.95 %	SLA 99.99%

For further details, you can visit the given URLs.
https://docs.microsoft.com/en-us/azure/virtual-machines/windows/manage-availability
https://social.technet.microsoft.com/wiki/contents/articles/51828.azure-vms-availability-sets-and-availability-zones.aspx

105. Answer: B

Explanation: Since an Availability Zone consists of one or more than one data centers, the answer is No. Because in the case of an Availability Zone with only one data center, we cannot ensure that, at any point in time, two virtual machines are always available in the event of a data center failure. From the point of best design standards, it is always advisable to have the VMs spread across multiple availability zones.

For further details, you can visit the given URL.
https://docs.microsoft.com/en-us/azure/availability-zones/az-overview

106. Answer: A

Explanation: Yes, this is the right approach. The Microsoft documentation mentions the following.

The fault domain and update domain make up the availability zone of an Azure region. You may effectively distribute your virtual machines across three fault domains and three update domains if you build three or more virtual machines in an Azure region spanning three zones. The Azure platform recognizes this distribution across update domains to make sure that VMs in separate zones are not scheduled to be upgraded at the same time.

For further details, you can visit the given URL.
https://docs.microsoft.com/en-us/azure/availability-zones/az-overview

107. **Answer: D**

Explanation: For an Azure Web App, you need to have an Azure App Service Plan in place. To minimize costs, you can have a single App Service Plan and link all the Azure Web Apps to that App Service Plan.

For further details, you can visit the given URL.

https://docs.microsoft.com/en-us/azure/app-service/overview-hosting-plans

108. Answer: B

Explanation: We are talking about an HTTP probe that requires a probe on a specified path in this problem. Because the relative path is /Temp, we need to ensure a file in this path on the virtual machines.

All other options are incorrect.

For further details, you can visit the given URL.

https://docs.microsoft.com/en-us/azure/load-balancer/load-balancer-custom-probe-overview

109. Answer: B

Explanation: Since the policy **Not allowed resource type** is assigned at the "**Subscription**" level, all the resources that belong to it will get impacted. Due to this reason, a virtual network cannot be created in **ipsgrpA** resource group.

For further details, you can visit the given URL.

https://docs.microsoft.com/en-us/azure/governance/policy/overview#assignments

110. Answer: B

Explanation: A policy is defined at the subscription level with a Deny permission on virtualNetworks. This becomes the permission rule for all resource groups in the subscription.

For further details, you can visit the given URL.

https://docs.microsoft.com/en-us/azure/governance/policy/overview

111. Answer: B

Explanation: The virtual machines need to be part of a virtual network. There is a policy definition not to allow virtual networks assigned to Staging Subscription. Since the "parent" is assigned this policy, we cannot have a virtual network created, and since VNET is there, the creation of the virtual machine will not be allowed in any of the resource groups.

For further details, you can visit the given URL.

https://docs.microsoft.com/en-us/azure/governance/policy/overview

112. Answer: B

Explanation: Even though ipsvm1 is in the Stopped (deallocated) state, this would still count the total number of vCPUs in the region. Hence adding a virtual machine with 16 vCPUs would cross the limit on vCPUs for the region.

You can easily find the subscription limit of vCPUs for the region using, for example, the following PowerShell command for the "West US" region: Get-AzVMUsage -Location "West US".

Quota is calculated based on the total number of cores in use both allocated and deallocated. If you need additional cores, request a quota increase or delete VMs that are no longer needed.

For further details, you can visit the given URL.

https://docs.microsoft.com/en-us/azure/azure-resource-manager/management/azure-subscription-service-limits

https://docs.microsoft.com/en-us/azure/virtual-machines/windows/quotas

113. Answer: A

Explanation: Since the total number of vCPUs comes within the limit, one would be able to create a virtual machine of this size. You can easily find the subscription limit of vCPUs for the region using, for example, the following PowerShell command for the "West US" region: Get-AzVMUsage -Location "West US".

For further details, you can visit the given URL.

https://docs.microsoft.com/en-us/azure/azure-resource-manager/management/azure-subscription-service-limits

114. Answer: C

Explanation: We can provide the Storage File Data SMB Share Reader RBAC role for this level of access.

The Microsoft documentation mentions the following.

To access Azure Files resources with identity-based authentication, an identity (a user, group, or service principal) must have the necessary permissions at the share level. This process is similar to specifying Windows share permissions, where you specify the type of access a particular user has to a file share. The guidance in this section demonstrates how to assign read, write, or delete permissions for a file share to an identity.

We have introduced three Azure built-in roles for granting share-level permissions to users:

- **Storage File Data SMB Share Reader** allows read access in Azure Storage file shares over SMB.

- **Storage File Data SMB Share Contributor** allows read, write, and delete access in Azure Storage file shares over SMB.
- **Storage File Data SMB Share Elevated Contributor** allows read, write, delete, and modifying NTFS permissions in Azure Storage file shares over SMB.

Since this is clearly given in the Microsoft documentation, all other options are incorrect.

For further details, you can visit the given URL.

https://docs.microsoft.com/en-us/azure/storage/files/storage-files-identity-auth-active-directory-domain-service-enable

115. Answer: D

Explanation: We can provide the Storage File Data SMB Share Elevated Contributor RBAC role for this level of access.

The Microsoft documentation mentions the following.

To access Azure Files resources with identity-based authentication, an identity (a user, group, or service principal) must have the necessary permissions at the share level. This process is similar to specifying Windows share permissions, where you specify the type of access a particular user has to a file share. The guidance in this section demonstrates how to assign read, write, or delete permissions for a file share to an identity.

We have introduced three Azure built-in roles for granting share-level permissions to users:

- **Storage File Data SMB Share Reader** allows read access in Azure Storage file shares over SMB.
- **Storage File Data SMB Share Contributor** allows read, write, and delete access in Azure Storage file shares over SMB.
- **Storage File Data SMB Share Elevated Contributor** allows read, write, delete, and modifying NTFS permissions in Azure Storage file shares over SMB.

Since this is clearly given in the Microsoft documentation, all other options are incorrect.

For further details, you can visit the given URL.

https://docs.microsoft.com/en-us/azure/storage/files/storage-files-identity-auth-active-directory-domain-service-enable

116. Answer: A

Explanation: The minimum number of backup policies required is "1," i.e., Option A reason using one single policy, we can have a backup of 100 VMs, and in our scenario, we have 2 VMs with a web application. Coming to the database, we do not need to define any policy.

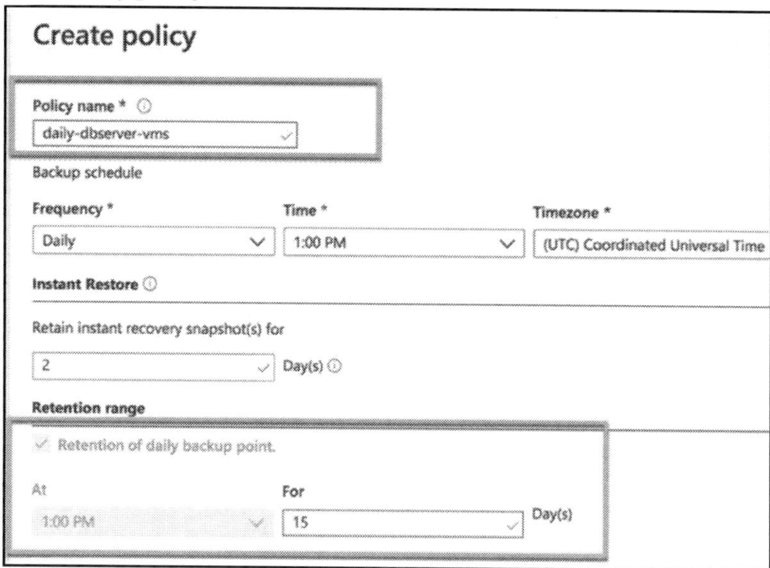

For further details, you can visit the given URL.
https://docs.microsoft.com/en-us/azure/backup/backup-azure-manage-vms

117. Answer: A

Explanation: Yes, you can. Even though the virtual machines and the Log Analytics workspace are in separate locations, you can still connect the virtual machines to the workspace.

For further details, you can visit the given URL.
https://docs.microsoft.com/en-us/azure/azure-monitor/learn/quick-collect-azurevm

118. Answer: B

Explanation: We will need to use Application collection rules for this.

The Microsoft documentation makes reference to the following.

Controlling outbound network access is a critical component of a comprehensive network security strategy. You might, for example, want to restrict access to certain websites. You could also want to restrict access to outbound IP addresses and ports.

Azure Firewall is one technique to manage outbound network access from an Azure subnet. You can configure Azure Firewall too:

- Application rules that define fully qualified domain names (FQDNs) can be accessed from a subnet.
- Network rules that define source address, protocol, destination port, and destination address.

Since this is mentioned in the Microsoft documentation, all other options are incorrect.

For further details, you can visit the given URL.

https://docs.microsoft.com/en-us/azure/firewall/tutorial-firewall-deploy-portal

119. Answer: A

Explanation:

Even though you have "Delete Lock" on ips-rg3, you still can move the web application "ips2050" but cannot delete the resources from this resource group.

For further detail, you can visit the given URL.

https://docs.microsoft.com/en-us/azure/azure-resource-manager/management/lock-resources

120. Answer: A

Explanation: Since the ipslabusr1 user has the role of Cloud Device Administrator and is a Group Owner, the user would be able to add registered or joined devices to the group.

For further detail, you can visit the given URL.

https://docs.microsoft.com/en-us/azure/active-directory/fundamentals/active-directory-accessmanagement-managing-group-owners

121. Answer: A

Explanation: You look at the comparison between the Standard and the Basic Load Balancer in the Microsoft documentation. It clearly mentions that virtual machines need to be a part of a single virtual network.

For further detail, you can visit the given URL.

https://docs.microsoft.com/en-us/azure/load-balancer/skus

122. Answer: D

Explanation: When transferring a large amount of data to an Azure storage account, you can transfer data to Azure blob storage or Azure file storage.

The Microsoft documentation mentions the following.

By sending disk drives to an Azure data center, the Azure Import/Export service is used to securely import huge amounts of data to Azure Blob storage and Azure Files. This service can also be used to transfer data from Azure Blob storage to disk drives, which can then be shipped to your on-premises installations. Data can be imported into Azure Files or Azure Blob storage from one or more hard disks.
For further detail, you can visit the given URL.
https://docs.microsoft.com/en-us/azure/import-export/storage-import-export-service

123. Answer: B
Explanation: Security questions are not asked during password resets for administrators under a specific policy.

For further details, you can visit the given URL.
https://docs.microsoft.com/en-us/azure/active-directory/authentication/concept-sspr-policy

124. Answer: B, D, and F
Explanation: For administrators, the password reset policy is different, wherein they are not asked security questions.
For further details, you can visit the given URL.
https://docs.microsoft.com/en-us/azure/storage/files/storage-sync-files-deployment-guide?tabs=portal

125. Answer: B
Explanation:
SLA for Virtual Machines:

For all Virtual Machines in the same Azure region with two or more instances deployed across two or more Availability Zones. We guarantee that at least one instance will have Virtual Machine Connectivity 99.99 percent of the time.

For all Virtual Machines with two or more instances deployed in the same Availability Set or the same Dedicated Host Group, we guarantee you will have Virtual Machine Connectivity to at least one instance at least 99.95% of the time.

For any Single Instance Virtual Machine using Premium SSD or Ultra Disk for all Operating System Disks and Data Disks, we guarantee you will have Virtual Machine Connectivity of at least 99.9%.

We guarantee Virtual Machine Connectivity of at least 99.5 percent for each Single Instance Virtual Machine using Standard SSD Managed Disks for the Operating System and Data Disks.
We guarantee Virtual Machine Connectivity of at least 95% for any Single Instance Virtual Machine employing Standard HDD Managed Disks for Operating System Disks and Data Disks.
For further detail, you can visit the given URL.
https://azure.microsoft.com/en-us/support/legal/sla/virtual-machines/v1_9/

126. Answer: E

Explanation:

If you look at the Network Contributor Role, it has access to manage Virtual Networks. And, of course, the Owner, by default, has all privileges over Azure resources.

For further detail, you can visit the given URL.
https://docs.microsoft.com/en-us/azure/role-based-access-control/built-in-roles#network-contributor

127. Answer: G

Explanation:

To work with the UNC path format, you have to mount the Azure file share with File Explorer.
For further detail, you can visit the given URL.
https://docs.microsoft.com/en-us/windows/win32/fileio/naming-a-file?redirectedfrom=MSDN

128. Answer: B

Explanation:

Since the policy is applied to the Tenant Root Group, it would be applied to all subscriptions and resource groups if you need to create a virtual machine. You must have permission to create virtual network resources required for VM provisioning. Hence the policy restricts the creation of Vnet resources. You wouldn't be able to create a new VM in this resource group.
For further detail, you can visit the given URL.
https://docs.microsoft.com/en-us/azure/governance/policy/overview

129. Answer: B

Explanation:

The virtual machine has to be in the Stopped or Deallocated state to replace the virtual machine's existing disks.

For further detail, you can visit the given URL.

https://docs.microsoft.com/en-us/azure/backup/backup-azure-arm-restore-vms#replace-existing-disks

130. Answer: B

Explanation:

Azure policies would only highlight the compliance of existing resources and enforce the policy restrictions on new resources. Hence the state of the virtual machine would remain as it is.

For further detail, you can visit the given URL.

https://docs.microsoft.com/en-us/azure/governance/policy/overview

131. Answer: A

Explanation:

We would be able to move the resource ipslabstore2090 from the resource group ipslabs-rg1 to ipslabs-rg2. The storage account ipslabstore2090 has a Delete lock. It means that we cannot delete this resource without removing the lock. But this lock does not prevent us from moving a resource from one resource group to another. The current ipslabstore2090 resource group, ipslabs-rg1, does not have any locks. The destination resource group ipslab-rg2, similar to the storage account, has a Delete lock. This lock prevents the deletion of this resource group and all resources within it. But it does not restrict the movement of the resources to this group from other groups.

For further detail, you can visit the given URL.

https://docs.microsoft.com/en-us/azure/azure-resource-manager/management/lock-resources?tabs=json

132. Answer: B

Explanation:

If you would not have added nsg-ipslab1 to SubnetA, then RDP to vmipdlab1 is possible. Since you have created a Windows VM, the RDP port is, by default, added to inbound rules.

In the given scenario, we are creating a new NSG called nsg-ipslab1, and it does not have an RDP port added to it. We need to get it added by creating a new rule.

Due to this reason, a "remote desktop" to vmips2 from vmipslab1 is not possible.

For further details, you can visit the given URL.

https://en.wikipedia.org/wiki/Remote_Desktop_Protocol

133. Answer: C

Explanation:

The Recovery Services vault and the virtual machine must be in the same region. This condition is fulfilled by the ipslabvm1, ipslabvm3, ipslabvmA, and ipslabvmC virtual machines. Because of the satisfaction of this condition, all other options are incorrect.

For further detail, you can visit the given URL.
https://docs.microsoft.com/en-us/azure/backup/backup-azure-vms-first-look-arm

134. Answer: C

Explanation:

To add a health probe, the user must have access to the "ipslab-public" load balancer. Out of the proposed options, only the Network Contributor role will provide such access. The other options are incorrect since they do not provide access to the "ipslab-public" load balancer.

For further detail, you can visit the given URL.
https://docs.microsoft.com/en-us/azure/role-based-access-control/overview

135. Answer: B

Explanation:

You have a duplicate file on the file share and the file server. The file on the file server will have its name appended with the name of the server.

For further detail, you can visit the given URL.
https://docs.microsoft.com/en-us/azure/storage/file-sync/file-sync-deployment-guide?tabs=azure-portal%2Cproactive-portal

136. Answer: B

Explanation:

In order to add the virtual machine to the virtual network, the virtual machine needs to be in the same region as the virtual network, which is not the case over here. The virtual machine is in the West US region, and the ipslabnetwork2 virtual network is in the East Asia region.

For further detail, you can visit the given URL.

https://docs.microsoft.com/en-us/azure/storage/file-sync/file-sync-deployment-guide?tabs=azure-portal%2Cproactive-portal

137. Answer: B

Explanation:

To protect the web servers against SQL injection attacks, one can use the Web Application Firewall feature. The Azure Online Application Firewall (WAF) on Azure Application Gateway protects your web applications from common exploits and vulnerabilities in a centralized manner. Malicious attacks on web applications that make use of well-known flaws are becoming more widespread. Among the most popular attacks are SQL injection and cross-site scripting.

For further detail, you can visit the given URL.

https://docs.microsoft.com/en-us/azure/web-application-firewall/ag/ag-overview

138. Answer: B

Explanation:

Each client machine that needs to establish a Point-to-Site VPN connection with the Azure virtual network must have the client certificate installed, and you must check this.

For further detail, you can visit the given URL.

https://docs.microsoft.com/en-us/azure/vpn-gateway/point-to-site-about

139. Answer: A

Explanation:

Even though there is a Read-only lock on the resource group, you can still move the web application to the target resource group. You cannot modify the properties of the resource group, but you can still move resources to the resource group.

For further detail, you can visit the given URL.

https://learn.microsoft.com/en-us/azure/azure-resource-manager/management/lock-resources

140. Answer: A

Explanation:

Since the lock type is a Delete lock, resources can still be added or updated in the resource group. Hence the Azure Web app can be moved to this resource group.

For further detail, you can visit the given URL.

https://docs.microsoft.com/en-us/azure/azure-resource-manager/management/move-resource-group-and-subscription

141. Answer: A

Explanation:

Since no resource locks are defined on this resource group, the web application can be moved to this resource group.

For further detail, you can visit the given URL.

https://docs.microsoft.com/en-us/azure/azure-resource-manager/management/move-limitations/app-service-move-limitations

142. Answer: B

Explanation:

To provide the ability to add the backend pool, the user must have the ability to read the details of the virtual machine and the virtual network. For this reason, the user needs to be given access at the resource group level. The other options are all invalid since they would only provide access to the load balancer resource itself and not provide access to the other resources, such as the virtual machines which needed to be added to the backend pool

For further detail, you can visit the given URL.

https://docs.microsoft.com/en-us/azure/role-based-access-control/built-in-roles#network-contributor

143. Answer: D

Explanation:

To add a health probe, the user needs to have access to the IP address of the virtual machine. And for this reason, the user also needs permission to read the details of the virtual machine. The other options are incorrect since they do not provide the relevant access to read the details of the virtual machine resource.

For further detail, you can visit the given URL.

https://docs.microsoft.com/en-us/azure/role-based-access-control/overview

144. Answer: A

Explanation:

Since the user is a group admin, the user can manage the group membership. The user would be able to add registered or joined devices to the group.

For further detail, you can visit the given URL.

https://docs.microsoft.com/en-us/azure/active-directory/fundamentals/active-directory-accessmanagement-managing-group-owners

145. Answer: A

Explanation:

Here the user has been given the Azure AD role of User Administrator. This role would allow the user to manage various aspects of the user and group administration.

For further detail, you can visit the given URL.

https://docs.microsoft.com/en-us/azure/active-directory/roles/permissions-reference

146. Answer: B

Explanation:

Since the group is Dynamic in nature, you will not be able to manually add users or devices to a group.

For further detail, you can visit the given URL.

https://docs.microsoft.com/en-us/azure/active-directory/fundamentals/active-directory-groups-create-azure-portal#group-and-membership-types

147. Answer: D

Explanation:

The virtual machines must be part of an availability set or a virtual machine scale set, according to the comparison between the Standard and Basic Load Balancer in the Microsoft specification.

For further detail, you can visit the given URL.

https://docs.microsoft.com/en-us/azure/load-balancer/

148. Answer: D

Explanation:

In the Microsoft documentation, the comparison between the Standard and Basic Load Balancers clearly states that the virtual machines must be part of a single virtual network.

For further detail, you can visit the given URL.

https://docs.microsoft.com/en-us/azure/load-balancer/

149. Answer: D

Explanation:

Here the Business Logic Tier has the requirement of NOT being accessible from the Internet. Hence, we should spin up an Internal Load Balancer.

For further detail, you can visit the given URL.

https://docs.microsoft.com/en-us/azure/virtual-machines/windows/tutorial-load-balancer#:~:text=An%20Azure%20load%20balancer%20is,incoming%20traffic%20among%20healthy%20VMs.&text=To%20distribute%20traffic%20to%20the,connected%20to%20the%20load%20balancer.

150. Answer: B

Explanation:

To protect the web servers against SQL injection attacks, one can use the Web Application Firewall feature.

The Azure Web Application Firewall (WAF) on Azure Application Gateway protects your web applications from common exploits and vulnerabilities in a centralized manner. Malicious attacks on web applications that make use of well-known flaws are becoming more widespread. Among the most popular attacks are SQL injection and cross-site scripting.

For further detail, you can visit the given URL.

https://docs.microsoft.com/en-us/azure/web-application-firewall/ag/ag-overview

151. Answer: A

Explanation:

In order to attach a network interface to a virtual machine, it must be created in the same region as the virtual machine and also be a part of the same virtual network hosting the virtual machine.

For further detail, you can visit the given URL.

https://docs.microsoft.com/en-us/azure/virtual-network/virtual-network-network-interface

152. Answer: A

Explanation:

In order to attach a network interface to a virtual machine, it must be created in the same region as the virtual machine and also be a part of the same virtual network hosting the virtual machine.

For further detail, you can visit the given URL.

https://docs.microsoft.com/en-us/azure/virtual-network/virtual-network-network-interface-vm

153. Answer: B

Explanation:

In order to attach a network interface to a virtual machine, it must be created in the same region as the virtual machine and also be a part of the same virtual network hosting the virtual machine.

For further detail, you can visit the given URL.

https://docs.microsoft.com/en-us/azure/virtual-network/virtual-network-network-interface

154. Answer: A

Explanation:

Here, the recovery services vault (ipslabvault1) is located in the Central US region. This means that only resources in this region can be backed up in the recovery services vault. And for this, we have only the virtual machine located in this region. Since this is the only approach for backing up data in the recovery services vault, all other options are incorrect

For further detail, you can visit the given URL.

https://docs.microsoft.com/en-us/azure/backup/backup-azure-recovery-services-vault-overview

155. Answer: B

Explanation:

Here the recovery services vault (ipslabvault2) is located in the West US region. This means that only resources in this region can be backed up in the recovery services vault.

Here we have the storage account in this region. Blob data cannot be backed up; we can only backup file shares in the recovery services vault.

Since this is the only approach for backing up data in the recovery services vault, all other options are incorrect

For further detail, you can visit the given URL.

https://docs.microsoft.com/en-us/azure/backup/backup-azure-recovery-services-vault-overview

156. Answer: C

Explanation:

When a device is joined to Azure AD, the user who joins the computer to the domain and any other Global and Cloud Device administrators are added as local administrators on the machine.

For further detail, you can visit the given URL.

https://docs.microsoft.com/en-us/azure/active-directory/roles/permissions-reference?WT.mc_id=Portal-Microsoft_AAD_IAM#device-administrators-permissions

157. Answer: B

Explanation:

If you have a duplicate file on the file share and the file server, the file on the file server will have its name appended with the name of the server. You will have the following files in the file share after adding the cloud endpoint and the first server endpoint.

For further detail, you can visit the given URL.

https://docs.microsoft.com/en-us/azure/storage/file-sync/file-sync-deployment-guide?tabs=azure-portal%2Cproactive-portal

158. Answer: B

Explanation:

If you have a duplicate file on the file share and the file server, the file on the file server will have its name appended with the name of the server.

After adding the cloud endpoint and the first server endpoint, you will have the following files on the server.

- ipslab1.txt
- ipslab1i-ipslabsrv1txt
- ipslab2.txt

For further detail, you can visit the given URL.

https://docs.microsoft.com/en-us/azure/storage/file-sync/file-sync-deployment-guide?tabs=azure-portal%2Cproactive-portal

159. Answer: A

Explanation:

Yes, after adding the second server endpoint, you will have the following files in place.

- ipslab1.txt
- ipslab1-ipslabsrv1txt
- ipslab2.txt

- ipslab2-ipslabsrv1.txt
- ipslab3.txt

For further detail, you can visit the given URL.

https://docs.microsoft.com/en-us/azure/storage/file-sync/file-sync-deployment-guide?tabs=azure-portal%2Cproactive-portal

160. Answer: D

Explanation:

When transferring data to an Azure storage account, you can transfer data to Azure blob storage or Azure file storage.

For further detail, you can visit the given URL.

https://docs.microsoft.com/en-us/azure/import-export/storage-import-export-service

161. Answer: B

Explanation:

For administrators, the password reset policy is different, wherein they are not asked security questions.

For further detail, you can visit the given URL.

https://docs.microsoft.com/en-us/azure/active-directory/authentication/concept-sspr-policy

162. Answer: B

Explanation:

For administrators, the password reset policy is different, wherein they are not asked security questions.

For further detail, you can visit the given URL.

https://docs.microsoft.com/en-us/azure/active-directory/authentication/concept-sspr-policy

163. Answer: A

Explanation:

Yes, since SSPR has been enabled for all users. The user would need to answer the security-related question to reset their password.

For further detail, you can visit the given URL.

https://docs.microsoft.com/en-us/azure/active-directory/authentication/concept-sspr-howitworks

164. Answer: D

Explanation:

For this, we have to configure Fraud alerts.

For further detail, you can visit the given URL.

https://cloudacademy.com/course/implementing-multi-factor-authentication/configure-fraud-alert/

165. Answer: B

Explanation:

The virtual machine must be in the same region as the virtual network in order to be added to the virtual network, which is not the case here.

The virtual machine is located in the West US, while the ipslabnetwork2 virtual network is located in East Asia.

For further detail, you can visit the given URL.

https://docs.microsoft.com/en-us/azure/virtual-machines/network-overview

166. Answer: A

Explanation:

Yes, this is the right approach. You will have to delete the virtual machine and then create the virtual machine in the East Asia region.

For further detail, you can visit the given URL.

https://docs.microsoft.com/en-us/azure/virtual-machines/network-overview

167. Answer: B

Explanation:

The virtual machine must be in the same region as the virtual network in order to be added to the virtual network, which is not the case here.

The virtual machine is located in the West US, while the ipslabnetwork2 virtual network is located in East Asia.

For further detail, you can visit the given URL.

https://docs.microsoft.com/en-us/azure/virtual-machines/network-overview

168. nswer: D

Explanation:

Since the networks are isolated from each other, you still need to ensure that the machines can communicate across the virtual networks. And this can be accomplished with the help of virtual network peering connections. Options A and

B are incorrect since service endpoints should be used when you want to connect virtual networks securely to other Azure-based services. Option C is incorrect since this should be used when you want to forward DNS requests to the Azure DNS servers.

For further detail, you can visit the given URL.

https://docs.microsoft.com/en-us/azure/virtual-network/virtual-network-peering-overview

169. Answer: D

Explanation:

Since you want to restore the folder on another virtual machine, you should install the Microsoft Azure Recovery Services Agent on the destination virtual machine.

Options A and B are incorrect since we want to restore the files using the Microsoft Azure Recovery Services Agent

Option C is incorrect. We already have the MARS agent running on this machine to take the backup.

For further detail, you can visit the given URL.

https://docs.microsoft.com/en-us/azure/backup/backup-windows-with-mars-agent

170. Answer: A

Explanation:

You can create alerts in Azure Monitor based on the events recorded in the Log Analytics workspace.

For further detail, you can visit the given URL.

https://docs.microsoft.com/en-us/azure/azure-monitor/alerts/alerts-log

171. Answer: B

Explanation:

You have to record the events in a Log Analytics workspace and then configure alerts in Azure monitor based on the Azure Log Analytics workspace.

For further detail, you can visit the given URL.

https://docs.microsoft.com/en-us/azure/azure-monitor/alerts/alerts-log

172. Answer: B

Explanation:

You have to record the events in a Log Analytics workspace. And then configure alerts in Azure monitor based on the Azure Log Analytics workspace.

For further detail, you can visit the given URL.
https://docs.microsoft.com/en-us/azure/azure-monitor/alerts/alerts-log

173. Answer: D
Explanation:
This can be accomplished with the Funnels feature of Application Insights.
For further detail, you can visit the given URL.
https://docs.microsoft.com/en-us/azure/azure-monitor/app/usage-funnels

174. Answer: A
Explanation:
This can be accomplished with the Impact feature of Application Insights.
For further detail, you can visit the given URL.
https://docs.microsoft.com/en-us/azure/azure-monitor/app/usage-impact

175. Answer: B
Explanation:
This can be accomplished with the Retention feature of Application Insights.
For further detail, you can visit the given URL.
https://docs.microsoft.com/en-us/azure/azure-monitor/app/usage-retention

176. Answer: B
Explanation:
This can be accomplished with the User Flows feature of Application Insights.
For further detail, you can visit the given URL.
https://docs.microsoft.com/en-us/azure/azure-monitor/app/usage-flows

177. Answer: B
Explanation:
You must verify that the client certificate is loaded on every client computer that needs to connect to the Azure virtual network via a Point-to-Site VPN connection.
For further detail, you can visit the given URL.
https://docs.microsoft.com/en-us/azure/vpn-gateway/point-to-site-about

178. Answer: B
Explanation:

You must verify that the client certificate is loaded on every client computer that needs to connect to the Azure virtual network via a Point-to-Site VPN connection.
For further detail, you can visit the given URL.

https://docs.microsoft.com/en-us/azure/vpn-gateway/point-to-site-about

179. Answer: A
Explanation:

The best approach is to install the client certificate on every machine that needs to access the Azure virtual network via a Point-to-Site VPN connection.
For further detail, you can visit the given URL.

https://docs.microsoft.com/en-us/azure/vpn-gateway/point-to-site-about

180. Answer: B
Explanation:

You must verify that the client certificate is loaded on every client computer that needs to connect to the Azure virtual network via a Point-to-Site VPN connection.
For further detail, you can visit the given URL.

https://docs.microsoft.com/en-us/azure/vpn-gateway/point-to-site-about

181. Answer: B
Explanation:
Here we first have to create the virtual network.

```
az network vnet create \
```

For further detail, you can visit the given URL.

https://docs.microsoft.com/en-us/azure/dns/private-dns-getstarted-cli

182. Answer: A
Explanation:
Next, you have to go ahead and create the private DNS zone.

For further detail, you can visit the given URL.

https://docs.microsoft.com/en-us/azure/dns/private-dns-getstarted-cli

183. Answer: D
Explanation:
Finally, you have to create a virtual network link for the zone.

For further detail, you can visit the given URL.

https://docs.microsoft.com/en-us/azure/dns/private-dns-getstarted-cli

184. Answer: C

Explanation:

The backup and restore option is available with the Standard App Service Plan.

	FREE	SHARED	BASIC	STANDARD	PREMIUM	ISOLATED*	APP SERVICE LINUX
64-bit			✓	✓	✓	✓	✓
App Service Advisor*			✓	✓	✓	✓	✓
Always On			✓	✓	✓	✓	
Authentication & Authorization	✓	✓	✓	✓	✓	✓	
Backup/Restore				✓	✓	✓	✓

Options A and B are incorrect since the backup and restore operation is unavailable with these App Service plans.

Option D is incorrect since this is not a cost-effective option

For further detail, you can visit the given URL.

https://azure.microsoft.com/en-us/pricing/details/app-service/windows/

185. Answer: C, D, and E

Explanation:

To record the successful and failed connection requests, we should use Azure Network Watcher flow logs. First, we can enable Network Watcher in the region of our choice and then use the Azure Network Watcher flow logs. The flow logs are then written to a storage account.

For further detail, you can visit the given URL.

https://docs.microsoft.com/en-us/azure/network-watcher/network-watcher-nsg-flow-logging-portal

186. Answer: B

Explanation:

The first step is to create a resource group. An Azure resource group is a logical group in which Azure resources are deployed and managed. When you create a resource group, you are asked to specify a location. This location is where resource group metadata is stored; it is also where your resources run in Azure if you do not

specify another region during resource creation. Create a resource group using the az group create command.

For further detail, you can visit the given URL.

https://docs.microsoft.com/en-us/azure/aks/kubernetes-walkthrough

187. Answer: C

Explanation:

The next step is to go ahead and create the Kubernetes cluster.

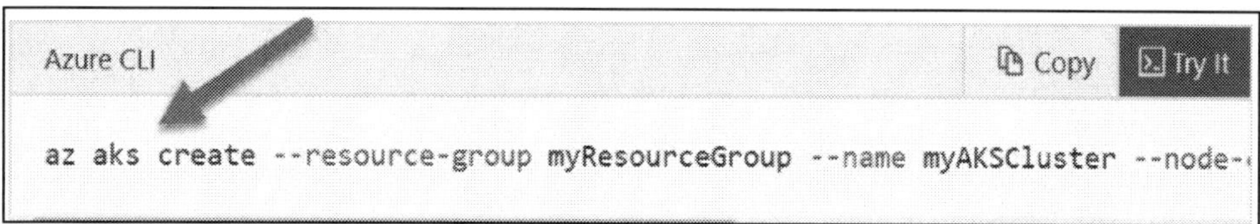

Since this is clearly mentioned in the Microsoft Documentation, all other options are incorrect.

For further detail, you can visit the given URL.

https://docs.microsoft.com/en-us/azure/aks/kubernetes-walkthrough

188. Answer: A

Explanation:

Since we have to ensure monitoring is enabled for the cluster, we have to use the --enable-addons switch.

An example of this is also given in the Microsoft documentation.

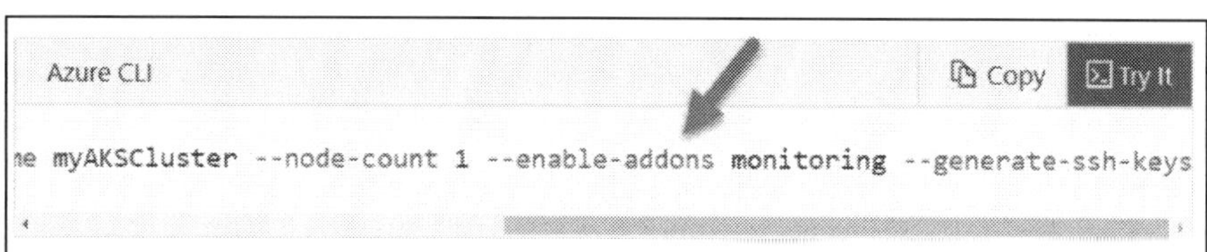

For further detail, you can visit the given URL.

https://docs.microsoft.com/en-us/azure/aks/kubernetes-walkthrough

189. Answer: B

Explanation:

Here you need to route traffic based on different URLs. Hence you should use a URL path-based routing rule

For further detail, you can visit the given URL.
https://docs.microsoft.com/en-us/azure/application-gateway/features

190. Answer: E
Explanation:
Here since we need to direct requests based on different sites, we need to use Multi-site listeners
For further detail, you can visit the given URL.
https://docs.microsoft.com/en-us/azure/application-gateway/features

191. Answer: B
Explanation:
For this requirement, you must create a service endpoint and configure network access to the storage account.
For further detail, you can visit the given URL.
https://docs.microsoft.com/en-us/azure/virtual-network/virtual-network-service-endpoints-overview

192. Answer: B
Explanation:
For this requirement, you must create a service endpoint and configure network access to the storage account.
For further detail, you can visit the given URL.
https://docs.microsoft.com/en-us/azure/virtual-network/virtual-network-service-endpoints-overview

193. Answer: A
Explanation:
Yes, this would fulfill the requirement. First, you should add a service endpoint for the virtual network and then ensure to limit the traffic from the virtual network to the storage account.

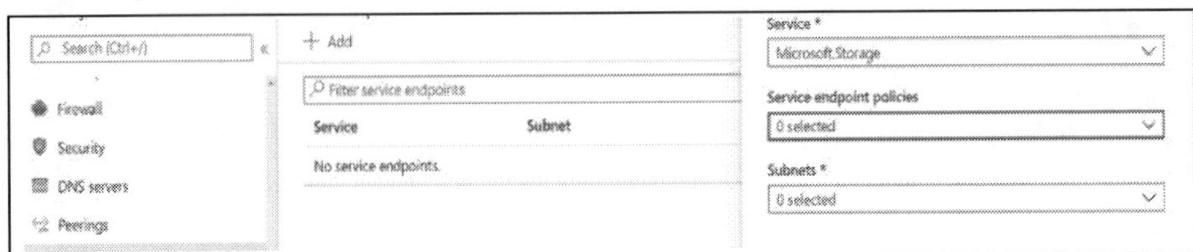

For further detail, you can visit the given URL.

https://docs.microsoft.com/en-us/azure/virtual-network/virtual-network-service-endpoints-overview

194. Answer: D

Explanation:

As per the case study, you have the following requirements

- Move the existing product blueprint files to Azure Blob storage.
- Copy the blueprint files to Azure over the Internet

You can easily copy files using the Azure Storage Explorer.

Options A and C are incorrect because this is used for File storage and not BLOB storage

Option B is incorrect since this is normally used as a one-time transfer of a large amount of data to Azure

For further detail, you can visit the given URL.

https://azure.microsoft.com/en-us/features/storage-explorer/

195. Answer: D

Explanation:

To back up any resource in Azure, the first thing you need to do is to create a Recovery Services vault.

For further detail, you can visit the given URL.

https://docs.microsoft.com/en-us/azure/backup/backup-azure-arm-vms-prepare

196. Answer: A

Explanation:

Since there is no requirement to have multiple virtual networks, one network would suffice for this requirement

For further detail, you can visit the given URL.

https://docs.microsoft.com/en-us/azure/virtual-network/virtual-networks-overview

197. Answer: C

Explanation:

Since there are 3 layers as part of the case study

- A SQL database
- A web front end
- Processing middle tier

It would be preferential to have a separate subnet for each layer.

For further detail, you can visit the given URL.

htt7s://docs.microsoft.com/en-us/azure/architecture/example-scenario/infrastructure/multi-tier-app-disaster-recovery

198. Answer: A and D

Explanation:

The Microsoft documentation mentions the following to support this:

- Users may join devices to Azure AD - This setting enables you to select the users who can join devices to Azure AD. The default is All. This setting is only applicable to Azure AD Join on Windows 10.
- Require Multi-Factor Authentication to join devices - You can choose whether users are required to provide a second authentication factor to join their device to Azure AD. The default is No. You recommend requiring multi-factor authentication when registering a device. Before you enable multi-factor authentication for this service, you must ensure that multi-factor authentication is configured for the users that register their devices.

Option B is incorrect since this is used for users that are granted local administrator rights on a device

Option C is incorrect since this setting is to allow devices to be registered with Azure AD

For further detail, you can visit the given URL.

https://docs.microsoft.com/en-us/azure/active-directory/devices/device-management-azure-portal

199. Answer: C

Explanation:

Suppose you have a Network Security group. Change the Incoming rules to allow port 443. This is so that users from the Internet can access the webserver on the secure port 443.

Options A and D are incorrect since users need to connect to the webserver, meaning the incoming rule needs to be modified and not the outgoing rules. Option B is incorrect since associating the Network Security Group with Multiple subnets will affect all the other tiers of the application.

For further detail, you can visit the given URL.

https://docs.microsoft.com/en-us/azure/virtual-network/security-overview

200. Answer: B, D, and F

Explanation:

These are the three basic steps you need to perform.

For further detail, you can visit the given URL.

https://docs.microsoft.com/en-us/azure/storage/file-sync/file-sync-deployment-guide?tabs=azure-portal%2Cproactive-portal

201. Answer: C, D, and E

Explanation:

The benefit of tagging and billing is given in the Microsoft documentation

Option A is incorrect since, here, the resources are used across various departments and are not constrained via a resource group

Option B is incorrect since the costing on a tag basis needs to be seen from the cost analysis

For further detail, you can visit the given URL.

https://docs.microsoft.com/en-us/azure/azure-resource-manager/management/tag-resources?tabs=json

202. Answer: C, E, and F

Explanation:

Since this is given in the documentation, all other options are incorrect

For further detail, you can visit the given URL.

https://docs.microsoft.com/en-us/azure/active-directory/fundamentals/add-custom-domain

203. Answer: B and C

Explanation:

These are the steps you need to perform to summarize your resource.

For further detail, you can visit the given URL.

https://azure.microsoft.com/en-us/support/legal/sla/load-balancer/v1_0/

204. Answer: C

Explanation:

Options A and B are incorrect since you do not need to recreate an entire load balancer just for this scenario; option D is incorrect since this is used to attach a front-end IP to the load balancer

For further detail, you can visit the given URL.

https://docs.microsoft.com/en-us/azure/load-balancer/tutorial-load-balancer-port-forwarding-portal

205. Answer: C

Explanation:

Option A is incorrect since this is used when you have multiple front-end IPs
Option B is incorrect since this is used to check the health of the back end VM's
Option D is incorrect since this is used for idle timeout
For further detail, you can visit the given URL.

https://docs.microsoft.com/en-us/azure/load-balancer/load-balancer-distribution-mode

206. Answer: B

Explanation:

If you go to your subscription and look at the Cost Analysis, you can see a breakdown of the costs for each resource.
The Cost Analysis section for the subscription allows you to see all the costs. Hence all other options are incorrect

For further detail, you can visit the given URL.

https://docs.microsoft.com/en-us/azure/cost-management/quick-acm-cost-analysis

207. Answer: B

Explanation:

The right solution is to use Network Watcher.
Data for Performance counters is collected using a data collector set.

For further detail, you can visit the given URL.

https://docs.microsoft.com/en-us/dynamics-nav/how-to--view-performance-counter-data-for-a-data-collector-set

208. Answer: A

Explanation:

The Microsoft documentation mentions the following:

By setting up packet capture sessions, you may use Network Watcher variable packet capture to track traffic to and from a virtual machine. Both reactively and proactively, packet capture aids in diagnosing network issues. Gathering network statistics is one of the other applications for obtaining data on network intrusions. To troubleshoot client-server connections, among other things.

For further detail, you can visit the given URL.
https://docs.microsoft.com/en-us/azure/network-watcher/network-watcher-packet-capture-overview

209. Answer: B

Explanation:

This is used to just see the number of packets coming into and out of the Virtual machine but will not do a detailed packet inspection.

For further detail, you can visit the given URL.
https://docs.microsoft.com/en-us/azure/azure-monitor/vm/monitor-vm-azure

210. Answer: A

Explanation:

Here you first have to get the role definition.

For further detail, you can visit the given URL.
https://docs.microsoft.com/en-us/azure/role-based-access-control/custom-roles-powershell

211. Answer: B

Explanation:

Here you first have to get the role definition.

For further detail, you can visit the given URL.
https://docs.microsoft.com/en-us/azure/role-based-access-control/custom-roles-powershell

212. Answer: B

Explanation:

Azure policies are used for governance purposes. The Microsoft documentation also gives an example of how you can use Azure policies to limit the use of SKUs for Azure virtual machines. Option A is incorrect since policies are used to control permissions at the resource property level. Option C is incorrect since Azure AD roles are specifically meant to control access to Azure AD. Option D is incorrect since there is no concept of subscription policies

For further detail, you can visit the given URL.
https://docs.microsoft.com/en-us/azure/governance/policy/overview

213. Answer: C

Explanation:

You can move Azure resources across subscriptions using the Move-AZ Resource PowerShell command. There are just some restrictions when moving Virtual Machines.
Option A is incorrect since you do not need to move the Virtual machine to any specific region for the move.
Option B is incorrect since you can move resources across subscriptions.
Option D is incorrect since the right command is Move-AZ Resource
For further detail, you can visit the given URL.
https://docs.microsoft.com/en-us/azure/virtual-machines/windows/move-vm

214. Answer: A
Explanation:
In order to add a network interface to a virtual machine, the machine needs to be stopped first.
For further detail, you can visit the given URL.
https://docs.microsoft.com/en-us/azure/virtual-network/virtual-network-network-interface-vm

215. Answer: B
Explanation:
The issue could be due to the security groups. You can diagnose the problem using IP Flow Verify.
Option A is incorrect since this is normally used from an application diagnostics perspective
Option C is incorrect since this is used to provide recommendations on various types of Azure resources
Option D is incorrect since this is used mainly from a security aspect in Azure
For further detail, you can visit the given URL.
https://docs.microsoft.com/en-us/azure/network-watcher/network-watcher-ip-flow-verify-overview

216. Answer: B
Explanation:
You can use the variable packet capture tool since it is the only tool that is helpful for checking on any network instructions.
For further detail, you can visit the given URL.
https://docs.microsoft.com/en-us/azure/network-watcher/network-watcher-packet-capture-manage-portal

217. nswer: A

Explanation:

The main issue is that the VM is not started and allocated an IP address. When you start the VM, you will get a public IP address assigned to the Network Interface. The Network security groups are fine for allowing RDP access.

Option B is incorrect because adding a new interface will not solve the connectivity issue

Options C and D are incorrect since you cannot delete the built-in network security group rules

For further detail, you can visit the given URL.

https://docs.microsoft.com/en-us/azure/virtual-network/security-overview

218. Answer: B

Explanation:

Option A is incorrect since this needs to be done for the currently attached network interface

Option C is incorrect since the incoming traffic needs to be allowed

Options D and E are incorrect since you cannot delete the built-in network security group rules

For further detail, you can visit the given URL.

https://docs.microsoft.com/en-us/azure/virtual-network/network-security-groups-overview

219. Answer: A

Explanation:

The other options are incorrect because these will not give the overall template deployment for multiple resources.

For further detail, you can visit the given URL.

https://docs.microsoft.com/en-us/azure/azure-resource-manager/templates/deploy-portal

220. Answer: C

Explanation:

Your IP address does not fit within the permitted IP address range specified by the SAS URL, hence access will be denied. All other selections are erroneous because this is the outcome of the SAS.

For further detail, you can visit the given URL.

https://docs.microsoft.com/en-us/azure/storage/common/storage-sas-overview

221. Answer: A

Explanation:

When we use net use, it does not support the use of Shared Access Signatures. Hence, we will not have access to the file share via the Shared Access Signature
For further detail, you can visit the given URL.

https://docs.microsoft.com/en-us/azure/storage/files/storage-how-to-use-files-windows#prerequisites

222. Answer: A

Explanation:

As a result, if you attach or have a network interface for a Virtual Machine, it might have both a private and public IP address.
As a result, you just need to define 5 network interface cards, one for each virtual machine, according to this method. As a result, all of the other choices are inaccurate.
For further detail, you can visit the given URL.

https://docs.microsoft.com/en-us/azure/virtual-network/virtual-network-network-interface

223. Answer: A

Explanation:

A network security group can have multiple network interfaces assigned to it. Since the question clearly states that the virtual machines all require the same inbound and outbound security rules, hence you should use just the same network security group for all network interfaces

For further detail, you can visit the given URL.

https://docs.microsoft.com/en-us/azure/virtual-network/virtual-network-vnet-plan-design-arm

224. Answer: C

Explanation:

The Virtual Network has no address space, which is relative to 192.168 10/24 as per the PowerShell output given in the Exhibit; after you save the address space, create a new subnet with the address space and then ensure the VM is put in the new subnet.

Option A is incorrect since the network interface can only receive an address from 10.2.0 0/24 as per the PowerShell output given in the Exhibit.
Option B is incorrect since you need to add the address space 192 168.1 0/24 before adding the subnet.
Options D and E are incorrect since you need to add the address space and subnet and not delete the address space and subnet.

For further detail, you can visit the given URL.

https://docs.microsoft.com/en-us/azure/virtual-network/virtual-networks-overview

225. Answer: B
Explanation:
You can add the new VM as part of the new subnet so that it receives the address from the 10.2.1.0/24 address space.
Option A is incorrect since the network interface can only receive an address from 10.2.0.0/24 as per the PowerShell output given in the Exhibit.
Option C is incorrect since you already have the required address space.

Options D and E are incorrect since you need to add the subnet and not delete the address space and subnet.
For further detail, you can visit the given URL.

https://docs.microsoft.com/en-us/azure/virtual-network/virtual-networks-overview

226. Answer: C, D, and E
Explanation:
To synchronize the files in the file share, you need to choose from these three options.

For further detail, you can visit the given URL.

https://docs.microsoft.com/en-us/azure/storage/file-sync/file-sync-deployment-guide?tabs=azure-portal%2Cproactive-portal

227. Answer: C
Explanation:
You can see that only General Purpose v2 supports all of the requirements. Hence all other options are incorrect

For further detail, you can visit the given URL.

https://docs.microsoft.com/en-us/azure/storage/common/storage-account-overview

228. Answer: C

Explanation:

Options A and B are incorrect since these replication strategies do not replicate the data across regions

Option D is inappropriate because it does not mention additional read access to data in another region, and you must also keep costs to a minimum.

For further detail, you can visit the given URL.

https://docs.microsoft.com/en-us/azure/storage/common/storage-redundancy

229. Answer: B

Explanation:

Scale sets are used to scale the Virtual machines based on load. But here, to achieve the desired level of availability, you also need to use an Availability set.

You can use availability sets along with scale sets to achieve high availability.

For further detail, you can visit the given URL.

https://azure.microsoft.com/en-us/support/legal/sla/virtual-machines/v1_9/

230. Answer: A

Explanation:

The Microsoft documentation mentions the following:

Configure multiple virtual machines in an availability set for redundancy.

To provide redundancy to your application, you recommend grouping two or more virtual machines in an availability set. This configuration within a data center ensures that during either a planned or unplanned maintenance event, at least one virtual machine is available and meets the 99.95% Azure SLA. For more information, see the SLA for Virtual Machines.

For further detail, you can visit the given URL.

https://docs.microsoft.com/en-us/azure/virtual-machines/windows/manage-availability

231. Answer: B

Explanation:

Using DNS queries, Azure Traffic Management distributes traffic. To achieve high availability,you need to use Availability sets.

For further detail, you can visit the given URL.

https://docs.microsoft.com/en-us/azure/traffic-manager/traffic-manager-overview

232. Answer: E

Explanation:

If you look at the Network Contributor Role, they have access to manage Virtual Networks. And then, by default, the Owner will have all privileges over Azure resources.

For further detail, you can visit the given URL.

https://docs.microsoft.com/en-us/azure/role-based-access-control/built-in-roles

233. Answer: A

Explanation:

The Network Contributor does not have access to assign roles. And if you look at the Security admin role, it only has the privilege of working with the Security Center.

For further detail, you can visit the given URL.

https://docs.microsoft.com/en-us/azure/role-based-access-control/built-in-roles#security-admin

234. Answer: B

Explanation:

If you look at the Microsoft documentation for the role definition, you can see that the correct action is *Microsoft.Authorization/'/read'.

For further detail, you can visit the given URL.

https://docs.microsoft.com/en-us/azure/role-based-access-control/built-in-roles

235. Answer: C

Explanation:

If you look at the Microsoft documentation for the role definition, you can see that the correct action is "Microsoft Support/**

For further detail, you can visit the given URL.

https://docs.microsoft.com/en-us/azure/role-based-access-control/built-in-roles

236. Answer: C

Explanation:

Vnet2 has an overlapping CIDR block, so Virtual Network peering cannot be established to this Virtual Network from VNet1

For further detail, you can visit the given URL.

https://docs.microsoft.com/en-us/azure/virtual-network/virtual-network-peering-overview

237. Answer: A

Explanation:

Since there are peerings in both directions for VNET1 and VNET3, the VMs can ping each other.

For further detail, you can visit the given URL.

https://docs.microsoft.com/en-us/azure/virtual-network/virtual-network-peering-overview

238. Answer: B

Explanation:

You must establish peerings in both directions for peering to function. So, this will not work.

For further detail, you can visit the given URL.

https://docs.microsoft.com/en-us/azure/virtual-network/virtual-network-peering-overview

239. Answer: B

Explanation:

If you look at the overall picture for the VNET peerings, VNET1 and VNET2 do not have any peering connection, so this will not work

For further detail, you can visit the given URL.

https://docs.microsoft.com/en-us/azure/virtual-network/virtual-network-peering-overview

240. Answer: F

Explanation:

The Archive access tier is only supported by the General Purpose V2 and Blob storage account types.

As a result, every other choice is erroneous.

For further detail, you can visit the given URL.

https://docs.microsoft.com/en-us/azure/storage/common/storage-account-overview

241. Answer: C

Explanation:

Since you do not want requests to flow via the Internet, you should create an internal load balancer.

Option A should not be used because it involves sending requests across the internet
Options B and D are incorrect terms when it comes to the load balancer
For further detail, you can visit the given URL.
https://docs.microsoft.com/en-us/azure/load-balancer/load-balancer-overview

242. Answer: A and C
Explanation:

Option B is the incorrect answer.

Having several network interfaces can be used to restore applications on virtual machines because network interfaces can be moved across virtual machines. However, you should employ a mix of Azure Managed Disks and Azure availability settings to ensure that you have an SLA of 99.5 percent uptime.

Option D is erroneous because it can be utilized to scale and provide high availability for your application. But we are here to make sure you get a 99.5 percent uptime guarantee. Azure Managed Disks and Azure availability sets should be used together.
For further detail, you can visit the given URL.
https://azure.microsoft.com/en-us/support/legal/sla/virtual-machines/v1_9/

243. Answer: C
Explanation:
When you add a custom domain name in Azure AD, you need to add it to your domain registrar to complete the registration of the custom domain.
Since this is clearly shown, all other options are invalid.
For further detail, you can visit the given URL.
https://docs.microsoft.com/en-us/azure/active-directory/fundamentals/add-custom-domain

244. Answer: B
Explanation:
Since the users will connect via HTTPS, that means that port 443 should be open. And you need to add an Inbound security rule.
Option A is incorrect since this is the port for HTTP traffic
Options C and D are incorrect since you need to modify the Inbound security rule
For further detail, you can visit the given URL.
https://docs.microsoft.com/en-us/azure/virtual-network/network-security-groups-overview

245. Answer: B

Explanation:

Joining devices to Azure AD reaps other benefits, as shown below. But it does not fulfill the current requirement. You can also join organization-owned devices to Azure AD. This mechanism offers the same benefits as registering a personal device with Azure AD. Additionally, users can sign in to the device using their corporate credentials.

For further detail, you can visit the given URL.

https://docs.microsoft.com/en-us/azure/vpn-gateway/vpn-gateway-howto-point-to-site-resource-manager-portal

246. Answer: B

Explanation:

The local VPN gateway is used when you want to define site-to-site VPN connections.

For further detail, you can visit the given URL.

https://docs.microsoft.com/en-us/azure/vpn-gateway/tutorial-site-to-site-portal

247. **Answer:** A and B

Explanation: By allowing attribute-based membership and resource access, groups that use dynamic membership rules lessen the administrative burden of access administration. The membership and ensuring access can be automatically given and removed based on membership rules.

For further details, you can visit the given URL.

https://learn.microsoft.com/en-us/azure/active-directory/enterprise-users/groups-dynamic-membership

248. **Answer:** D

Explanation: Users given the Global reader position are prohibited from making any alterations. The role is a read-only variant of Global administrator, allowing users to view settings and administrative data for all services but preventing them from performing management tasks.

For further details, you can visit the given URL.

https://learn.microsoft.com/en-us/azure/active-directory/roles/permissions-reference#global-reader

249. **Answer:** A

Explanation: A custom role can be exported as JSON and then imported into another custom role because creating custom roles in Azure can be complicated due to the thousands of rights available. The job must first be exported in JSON format. The information in the custom job can then be imported as a JSON file into a different tenant.

For further details, you can visit the given URL.

https://learn.microsoft.com/en-us/azure/role-based-access-control/custom-roles

250. **Answer:** A

Explanation: A collection of notification choices set by the owner of an Azure subscription makes up an action group. Action groups are used by Azure Monitor, Service Health, and Azure Advisor alerts to let users know when an alert has been activated.

For further details, you can visit the given URL.

https://learn.microsoft.com/en-us/azure/azure-monitor/alerts/action-groups

251. **Answer:** A and B

Explanation: You can build reports and dashboards for alerting, budgeting, and performance management by assigning Tags to Virtual Machines. Tags can be added using ARM templates, PowerShell, and the Azure CLI.

For further details, you can visit the given URL.

https://learn.microsoft.com/en-us/azure/cloud-adoption-framework/decision-guides/resource-tagging/

252. **Answer:** B

Explanation: Geo-Redundant Storage (GRS) uses LRS to duplicate your data thrice within a single physical location in the central area. Then, it makes an asynchronous copy of your data to a singular physical location hundreds of miles from the primary and secondary regions. Only LRS is supported by storage accounts set to the Premium performance option. It is impossible to immediately switch to another replication setting or change any storage accounts configured with ZRS. In this case, storage2 can be switched to geo-redundant storage and is the only storage account not configured to LRS or Premium performance.

For further details, you can visit the given URL.

https://learn.microsoft.com/en-us/azure/storage/common/storage-redundancy

253. **Answer:** B

Explanation: When deploying an Azure Resource Manager (ARM) template, you can take secrets from an Azure key vault and send them as parameters. Since you can only explicitly refer to the vital vault ID and not the credentials, the parameter value is never revealed.

For further details, you can visit the given URL.

https://learn.microsoft.com/en-us/azure/azure-resource-manager/templates/template-tutorial-use-key-vault

254. **Answer:** A

Explanation: Use the az group deletes command in the Azure CLI to deactivate a resource group. The -no-wait option instructs the open command prompt to skip long-running operations, and the -yes switch instructs the prompt to skip asking for confirmation.

For further details, you can visit the given URL.

https://learn.microsoft.com/en-us/cli/azure/group?view=azure-cli-latest#az_group_delete&preserve-view=true

255. **Answer:** D

Explanation: You should export a JSON template to create numerous Azure resources based on a single existing resource. A template can be exported from a resource, a resource group, or the deployment timeline. In this case, exporting the blueprint from the VM1 blade would be required.

If you wished to make an image of the current VM, you would use Capture. The original VM will become useless as a result, though. Before taking a VM image, there are several preparation chores to finish. Since these options handle failed connections or VM states, you wouldn't choose Redeploy + reapply. VM high availability is configured and managed using availability and scaling, no VMs are created based on predetermined setup settings.

For further details, you can visit the given URL.

https://learn.microsoft.com/en-us/azure/azure-resource-manager/templates/export-template-portal

256. **Answer:** B

Explanation: You must validate the name to confirm domain ownership when you add a custom domain to an App Service. Then, generate a text record containing the Custom Domain Verification ID to verify domain ownership for contoso.com. Using

the CNAME entry, http://www.contoso.com is mapped to webapp.azurewebsites.net.

For further details, you can visit the given URL.

/azure/app-service/app-service-web-tutorial-custom-domain?tabs=cname; /azure/app-service/manage-custom-dns-buy-domain

257. **Answer:** C

Explanation: You must change the critical vault's Access policies to implement Azure Disk Encryption. It gives users the option to allow access to volume encryption through Azure Disk Encryption.

For further details, you can visit the given URL.

https://learn.microsoft.com/en-us/azure/virtual-machines/windows/disk-encryption-key-vault

258. **Answer:** A and D

Explanation: Azure Virtual Machines, SQL in Azure VM, Azure Files, SAP HANA in Azure VM, Azure Backup Server, Azure Backup Agent, and DPM are all supported by Recovery Services storage. Azure Database for PostgreSQL servers, Azure Blobs, and Azure discs are all supported by Backup Vault.

For further details, you can visit the given URL.

/azure/backup/backup-support-matrix#vault-support; /azure/backup/backup-azure-recovery-services-vault-overview; /azure/backup/backup-vault-overview

259. **Answer:** C

Explanation: Assign tags to the virtual machines.

For further details, you can visit the given URL.

https://docs.microsoft.com/en-us/azure/azure-resource-manager/resource-group-using-tags

260. **Answer:** C

Explanation: Using the az vm create cmdlet and the --custom-data parameter to specify the complete path to the cloud-init.txt file, you can launch the VM after creating Cloud-init.txt.

For further details, you can visit the given URL.

https://docs.microsoft.com/en-us/azure/virtual-machines/linux/tutorial-automate-vm-deployment

261. **Answer:** B

Explanation: You must establish a new provider and reactivate your existing server using the activation credentials of the new provider because it is currently not feasible to change the usage model of an existing provider.

For further details, you can visit the given URL.

https://365lab.net/2015/04/11/switch-usage-model-in-azure-multi-factor-authentication-server/

262. **Answer:** B

Explanation: The usage model of an existing provider cannot be changed as it stands, so you must make a new one and reactivate your current server using the activation credentials of the new provider.

For further details, you can visit the given URL.

https://365lab.net/2015/04/11/switch-usage-model-in-azure-multi-factor-authentication-server/

263. **Answer:** A

Explanation: An existing provider's usage model cannot be changed as it stands, so you must make a new provider and reactivate your current server using the activation credentials of the new provider.

For further details, you can visit the given URL.

https://365lab.net/2015/04/11/switch-usage-model-in-azure-multi-factor-authentication-server/

264. **Answer:** B

Explanation: As read-only access to the data replicated to the secondary location is provided by RA-GRS, you can have greater read availability for your storage account. If the data is not accessible in the primary region after you enable this feature, you may use the secondary location to achieve greater availability. This function is opt-in and necessitates geo-replication of the storage account.

For further details, you can visit the given URL.

https://docs.microsoft.com/en-us/azure/storage/common/storage-redundancy

265. **Answer:** B

Explanation: Use the Resource Group blade.

For further details, you can visit the given URL.

https://docs.microsoft.com/en-us/azure/azure-resource-manager/resource-manager-export-template

266. **Answer:** A

Explanation: To see a blueprint from a previous deployment:

1. Visit your new resource group's resource group. Take note that the portal displays the outcome of the most recent launch. Choose this URL.

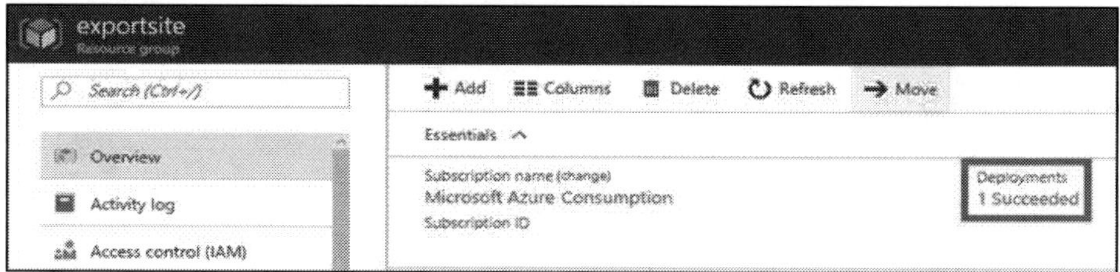

2. You can view the group's deployment records. The portal most likely only shows one launch in your situation. Decide to use this implementation.

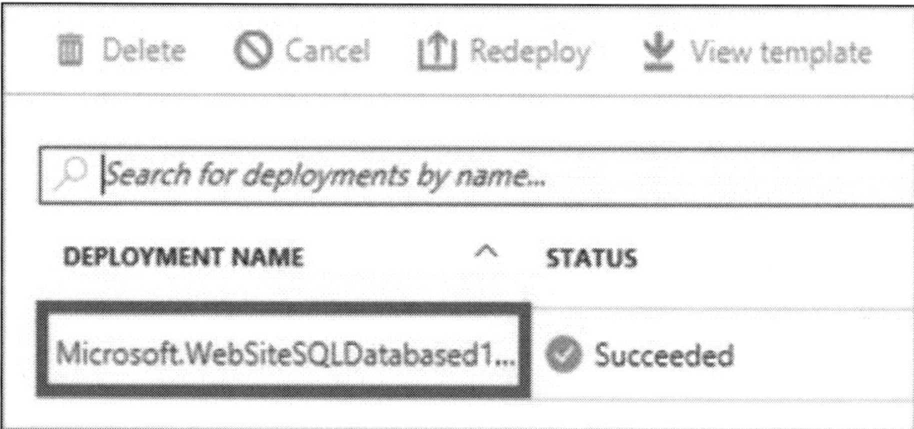

3. A summary of the rollout is shown on the portal. The deployment status, the state of its activities, and the parameter values you supplied are all included in the summary. Select View template to view the design you used for the deployment.

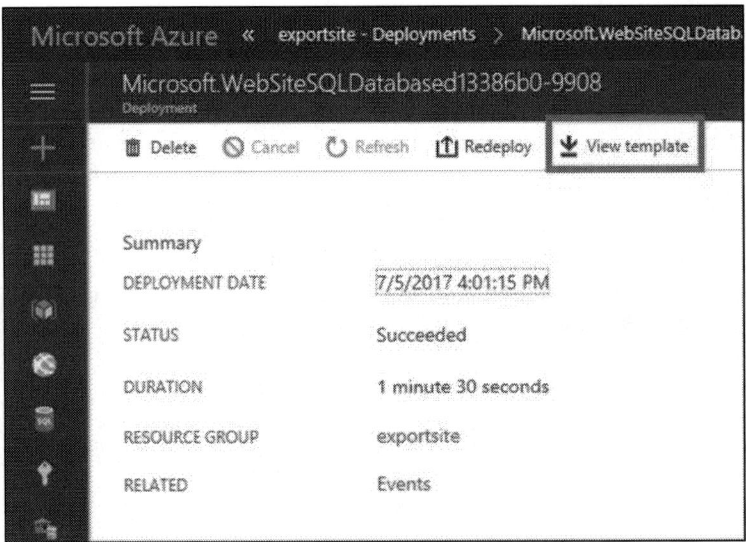

For further details, you can visit the given URL.

https://docs.microsoft.com/en-us/azure/azure-resource-manager/resource-manager-export-template

267. **Answer:** B

Explanation: Use the Resource Group blade.

For further details, you can visit the given URL.

https://docs.microsoft.com/en-us/azure/azure-resource-manager/resource-manager-export-template

268. **Answer:** C

Explanation: When changing the size of a VM member of an availability set, you must first halt all of the other VMs in the availability set.

Because every running VM in the availability set needs to be using the same physical hardware cluster, all of them must be stopped before conducting the resize operation to a size that requires different hardware. Therefore, all VMs must first be stopped and then individually restarted to another physical hardware cluster if a change in the physical hardware cluster is necessary to alter the VM size.

For further details, you can visit the given URL.

https://azure.microsoft.com/es-es/blog/resize-virtual-machines/

269. **Answer:** A

Explanation: Stop the virtual machine that contains the data disc.

For further details, you can visit the given URL.

https://docs.microsoft.com/en-us/azure/virtual-machines/windows/detach-disk
https://docs.microsoft.com/en-us/azure/lab-services/devtest-lab-attach-detach-data-disk

270. **Answer:** D

Explanation: There are typically two or three fault domains per area for managed availability sets.

For further details, you can visit the given URL.

https://docs.microsoft.com/en-us/azure/virtual-machines/windows/manage-availability

271. **Answer:** B

Explanation: Each virtual machine in your availability group receives an update and failure domain from the Azure infrastructure that underlies it. Five non-user-configurable update domains, or groups of virtual machines and underlying physical hardware that can reboot simultaneously, are allocated by default for a given availability set (Resource Manager deployments can then be expanded to provide up to 20 update domains).

For further details, you can visit the given URL.

https://docs.microsoft.com/en-us/azure/virtual-machines/availability-set-overview

272. **Answer:** A

Explanation: A virtual machine must be modified after deployment before it is ready for use. You can do this directly or, for example, automate the configuration of your VM after deployment using Remote PowerShell.

However, CustomScriptextension is now a third option to customize your VM.

The VM Agent runs this CustomScript extension, which is very simple. You tell it which files to obtain from your storage account and which files to run. Even the arguments that must be given to the script can be specified. You only need to run the a.ps1 file as a prerequisite.

For further details, you can visit the given URL.

https://docs.microsoft.com/en-us/windows-hardware/manufacture/desktop/add-a-custom-script-to-windows-setup https://azure.microsoft.com/en-us/blog/automating-vm-customization-tasks-using-custom-script-extension/

273. **Answer:** B

Explanation: On-premises virtual hard discs in the.vhd file format are transferred to a blob storage account as fixed virtual hard discs using the Add-AzVhd command.

For further details, you can visit the given URL.

https://docs.microsoft.com/en-us/azure/virtual-machines/windows/upload-generalized-managed

274. **Answer:** C

Explanation: You can establish a secure link to your virtual network from a single client computer using a Point-to-Site (P2S) VPN gateway connection.

For further details, you can visit the given URL.

https://docs.microsoft.com/en-us/azure/vpn-gateway/vpn-gateway-about-vpngateways

275. **Answer:** E

Explanation: Choose a static internal IP for a VM that has already been established.

The following cmdlets can assign a static IP address to a virtual machine you previously established. Before using these cmdlets, you must remove the current static IP address from the VM if you have already assigned it an IP address and want to modify it. To delete a static IP, follow the directions below.

You will use the Update-AzureVM cmdlet for this process. The upgrade-AzureVM cmdlet restarts the virtual machine as part of the upgrade procedure. After the VM restarts, the DIP that you designate will be assigned. In this illustration, we'll establish VM2's IP address housed in the cloud service StaticDemo.

Get-AzureVM -ServiceName StaticDemo -Name VM2 | Set-AzureStaticVNetIP -IPAddress 192.168.4.7 | Update-AzureVM

For further details, you can visit the given URL.

https://learn.microsoft.com/en-us/azure/virtual-network/ip-services/virtual-networks-static-private-ip-classic-ps

276. **Answer:** A

Explanation: 5

Azure Active Directory (Azure AD) is a service your business subscribes to.

Five Virtual Machines (VMs) must be deployed to the virtual network subnet of your business. Therefore, the configurations requires the fewest number of network interfaces will also be the same.

For further details, you can visit the given URL.

https://learn.microsoft.com/en-us/azure/virtual-network/ip-services/associate-public-ip-address-vm

277. **Answer:** D

Explanation: 1

Azure Active Directory (Azure AD) is a service your business subscribes to.

Five Virtual Machines (VMs) must be deployed to the virtual network subnet of your business.

Each VM will have a private and public IP address. The inbound and outbound security protocols must be identical for each virtual machine. For this, the configurations requires the fewest security groups should be 1.

For further details, you can visit the given URL.

https://learn.microsoft.com/en-us/azure/virtual-network/network-overview

278. **Answer:** A

Explanation: Only the infected VM can be used to recover the data.

https://learn.microsoft.com/en-us/azure/security/fundamentals/backup-plan-to-protect-against-ransomware

279. **Answer:** B

Explanation: Any VM included in the company's subscription should be used to recover the VM.

For further details, you can visit the given URL.

https://learn.microsoft.com/en-us/azure/azure-resource-manager/management/move-limitations/virtual-machines-move-limitations

280. **Answer:** B

Explanation: The time-series database that keeps metrics in Azure Monitor is designed for time-stamped data analysis. Metrics are exceptionally well adapted for alerting and quick issue detection.

For further details, you can visit the given URL.

https://docs.microsoft.com/en-us/azure/azure-monitor/platform/data-platform

281. **Answer:** A, B, C, D, and E

Explanation: Windows Server 2008's 64-bit operating system can be backed up using Azure Backup.

Windows 10 64-bit copy is supported by Azure copy.

Debian 64-bit operating systems starting with Debian 7.9 and later, are supported by Azure Backup.

Azure Backup allows for the Backup of offline or turned-down virtual machines.

For further details, you can visit the given URL.

https://docs.microsoft.com/en-us/azure/backup/backup-support-matrix-iaas
https://docs.microsoft.com/en-us/azure/virtual-machines/linux/endorsed-distros

282. **Answer:** B

Explanation: A account is created in Azure Active Directory (Azure AD) using the New-AzureADUser cmdlet.

To welcome a new external user to your directory, use the New-AzureADMSInvitation cmdlet instead.

For further details, you can visit the given URL.

https://docs.microsoft.com/en-us/powershell/module/azuread/new-azureadmsinvitation

283. **Answer:** B

Explanation: To welcome a new external user to your directory, use the New-AzureADMSInvitation cmdlet instead.

For further details, you can visit the given URL.

https://docs.microsoft.com/en-us/powershell/module/azuread/new-azureadmsinvitation

284. **Answer:** A

Explanation: To add a new outside user to your directory, use the New-AzureADMSInvitation command.

For further details, you can visit the given URL.

https://docs.microsoft.com/en-us/powershell/module/azuread/new-azureadmsinvitation

285. **Answer:** B

Explanation: Create an OAuth 2.0 authentication endpoint from contoso.com.

For further details, you can visit the given URL.

https://kubernetes.io/docs/reference/access-authn-authz/authentication/

286. **Answer:** A and C

Explanation: In Azure Active Directory (Azure AD), you can only establish an expiration policy for Office 365 groups.

Note: Administrators and users need a method to eliminate unused groups due to the increased use of Office 365 Groups. Expiration rules can help the system become cleaner by removing inactive groups.

A group's related services, such as the mailbox, Planner, SharePoint site, etc., are also deleted when a group ends.

On security groups or Office 365 groups, you can configure a rule for active participation.

For further details, you can visit the given URL.

https://docs.microsoft.com/en-us/office365/admin/create-groups/office-365-groups-expiration-policy?view=o365-worldwide

287. **Answer:** B

Explanation: Except for ContosoRG1, you cannot create Azure SQL servers anywhere in Subscription 1.

For further details, you can visit the given URL.

https://learn.microsoft.com/en-us/answers/questions/531260/cannot-create-azure-sql-server

288. **Answer:** C

Explanation: Run the Set-AzMarketplaceTerms command in Azure PowerShell.

For further details, you can visit the given URL.

https://docs.microsoft.com/en-us/powershell/module/az.marketplaceordering/set-azmarketplaceterms?view=azps-4.1.0

289. **Answer:** B

Explanation: Assign a user a position -

1. Log in to the Azure interface using a user account with the directory's global admin or privileged role admin privileges.
2. Choose Users from the list under Azure Active Directory, then pick a particular user from the list.
3. Choose the suitable admin roles from the Directory roles list, such as Conditional access administrator, and then click Add a role for the chosen user.
4. To save, press Select.

For further details, you can visit the given URL.

https://docs.microsoft.com/en-us/azure/active-directory/fundamentals/active-directory-users-assign-role-azure-portal

290. **Answer:** A

Explanation: Assign a license using the Azure AD's Licenses component.

For further details, you can visit the given URL.

https://docs.microsoft.com/en-us/azure/active-directory/fundamentals/license-users-groups

291. **Answer:** C

Explanation: You can connect Azure and a supported IT application Management (ITSM) product or application, such as Microsoft System Center Service Manager, using the IT Service Management Connector (ITSMC).

Based on your Azure alerts, you can generate work items in the ITSM tool using ITSMC (metric alerts, Activity Log alerts, and Log Analytics alerts).

For further details, you can visit the given URL.

https://docs.microsoft.com/en-us/azure/azure-monitor/platform/itsmc-overview

292. **Answer:** A

Explanation: The following security guidelines are added to the local administrator's group on the connected Windows computer by Azure AD when you use an Azure AD join:

- The global administrator position in Azure AD
- The device administrator position in Azure AD
- the person who executes the Azure AD merge

On the Devices page of the Azure portal, you can manage the device administrator position. For the Devices tab to load:

1. Log into your Azure portal as a global user or device administrator.
2. Select Azure Active Directory from the left navbar.
3. Choose Devices from the Manage area.
4. Click Device settings on the Devices tab.
5. On devices that have joined Azure AD, configure Additional local administrators to change the device administrator position.

For further details, you can visit the given URL.

https://docs.microsoft.com/en-us/azure/active-directory/devices/assign-local-admin

293. **Answer:** B

Explanation: The full access to all resources, including the authority to grant others entry.

There are two suitable responses to the query:

- For VNet1, give User1 the User Access Administrator job
- Give User1 the VNet1 Owner position

The following are some additional wrong response choices you might come across on the test:

- For VNet1, give User1 the Contributor status
- For Subscription1, remove User1 from the Security Reader and Reader responsibilities. For Subscription1, give User1 the Contributor status
- Assign User1 the Contributor role for RG1. Remove User1 from the Security Reader position for Subscription1

For further details, you can visit the given URL.

https://docs.microsoft.com/en-us/azure/role-based-access-control/overview

294. **Answer:** A

Explanation: To confirm your personal domain name (example)

1. Log into the Azure interface using a Global administrator account for the directory.

2. Select Custom domain names after choosing Azure Active Directory.

3. Choose the Contoso custom domain name from the list on the Fabrikam - Custom domain names website.

4. Select Verify on the Contoso screen to confirm that your custom domain has been correctly registered and is valid for Azure AD. Use the MX record type or the TXT record type.

Note: The question can have two potential answers:

1. MX

2. TXT

Other incorrect response choices for the query include the following:

1. SRV

2. NSEC3

For further details, you can visit the given URL.

https://docs.microsoft.com/en-us/azure/dns/dns-web-sites-custom-domain

295. **Answer:** B

Explanation: You can only link to, initiate, restart, and shut down virtual machines in your Azure DevTest Labs using the DevTest Labs User role.

You can administer logic apps with the Logic App Contributor role but can't access them. A logic program can be accessed, edited, and updated.

For further details, you can visit the given URL.

https://docs.microsoft.com/en-us/azure/role-based-access-control/built-in-roles
https://docs.microsoft.com/en-us/azure/logic-apps/logic-apps-securing-a-logic-app

296. **Answer:** B

Explanation: The Logic App Contributor position would be required.

For further details, you can visit the given URL.

https://docs.microsoft.com/en-us/azure/role-based-access-control/built-in-roles
https://docs.microsoft.com/en-us/azure/logic-apps/logic-apps-securing-a-logic-app

297. **Answer:** A

Explanation: The Contributor position can manage all resources (and new ones) in a resource group.

For further details, you can visit the given URL.

https://learn.microsoft.com/en-us/azure/azure-resource-manager/management/manage-resource-groups-portal

298. **Answer:** B

Explanation: After the search operator, add the table name to look for a term in a specific table.

Note: There are two suitable responses to the query:

1. Event | search "error"
2. Event | where EventType == "error"
3. search in (Event) "error"

The following are some additional wrong response choices you might come across on the test:

1. Get-Event Event | where {$_.EventTye â€"eq "error"}

2. Event | where EventType is "error"
3. search in (Event) * | where EventType â€"eq "error"
4. select * from Event where EventType is "error"

For further details, you can visit the given URLs.

https://docs.microsoft.com/en-us/azure/azure-monitor/log-query/search-queries https://docs.microsoft.com/en-us/azure/azure-monitor/log-query/get-started-portal https://docs.microsoft.com/en-us/azure/data-explorer/kusto/query/searchoperator?pivots=azuredataexplorer

299. **Answer:** A and E

Explanation: An internal load balancer directs network traffic from the VPN gateway to the cloud service. The front-end subnet of the program is where the load balancer is situated.

For further details, you can visit the given URLs.

https://docs.microsoft.com/en-us/azure/architecture/reference-architectures/hybrid-networking/vpn https://docs.microsoft.com/en-us/azure/load-balancer/load-balancer-overview https://docs.microsoft.com/en-us/azure/application-gateway/overview

300. **Answer:** B

Explanation: By locating idle and underutilized resources, Advisor assists you in optimizing and lowering your total Azure expenditure. On the Advisor dashboard, click the Cost tab to receive cost suggestions.

For further details, you can visit the given URL.

https://docs.microsoft.com/en-us/azure/advisor/advisor-cost-recommendations

301. **Answer: A**

Explanation: Edit the External collaboration options in the Users settings blade.

For further details, you can visit the given URL.

https://techcommunity.microsoft.com/t5/Azure-Active-Directory/Generic-authorization-exception-inviting-Azure-AD-gests/td-p/274742

302. **Answer:** B

Explanation: The list of roles and the allowed actions for management groups are displayed in the chart below.

Azure Role Name	Create	Rename	Move**	Delete	Assign Access	Assign Policy	Read
Owner	X	X	X	X	X	X	X
Contributor	X	X	X	X			X
MG Contributor*	X	X	X	X			X
Reader							X
MG Reader*							X
Resource Policy Contributor						X	
User Access Administrator					X	X	

Note: The "Root" management group is the only top-level management group assigned to each location. All management groups and subscriptions will fold up to this core management group, built into the hierarchy. Global policies and Azure job assignments can be implemented at the directory level due to this root management group. The Azure AD Global Administrator must first attain this root group's User Access Administrator position. To handle the hierarchy, the administrator can grant any Azure role to additional directory users or groups after elevating access. You can designate your account as the root management group's owner in your capacity as supervisor.

For further details, you can visit the given URL.

https://docs.microsoft.com/en-us/azure/governance/management-groups/overview

303. **Answer:** A

Explanation: Enable traffic monitoring, one of the following conditions must be met by your account:

Any one of the following Azure roles - owner, contributor, reader, or network contributor - must be assigned to your user at the subscription scope.

For further details, you can visit the given URL.

https://docs.microsoft.com/en-us/azure/network-watcher/traffic-analytics-faq

304. **Answer:** A

Explanation: To activate traffic analytics, your account must fulfill one of the requirements listed below:

The owner, contributor, reader, or network contributor Azure responsibilities are required for your account at the subscription scope.

For further details, you can visit the given URL.

https://docs.microsoft.com/en-us/azure/network-watcher/traffic-analytics-faq

305. **Answer:** A

Explanation: Enable traffic monitoring, one of the following requirements must be met by your account:

Any of the following Azure roles - owner, contributor, reader, or network contributor - must be assigned to your account at the start of your subscription.

For further details, you can visit the given URL.

https://docs.microsoft.com/en-us/azure/network-watcher/traffic-analytics-faq

306. **Answer:** C

Explanation: Contributor: Provides complete control over all resources but prevents job assignment in Azure RBAC

For further details, you can visit the given URL.

https://docs.microsoft.com/en-us/azure/role-based-access-control/built-in-roles%20https:/docs.microsoft.com/en-us/azure/logic-apps/logic-apps-securing-a-logic-app

307. **Answer:** A

Explanation: Azure services have an automatically managed name in Azure Active Directory thanks to managed identities for Azure resources. You can use this identity without requiring credentials in your code to log in to any Azure AD authentication service.

You can activate and disable the system-assigned managed identity for VM using the Azure portal.

For further details, you can visit the given URL.

https://docs.microsoft.com/en-us/azure/active-directory/managed-identities-azure-resources/qs-configure-portal-windows-vm

308. **Answer:** A

Explanation: You must set up a Name Server (NS) entry for the zone.

For further details, you can visit the given URL.

https://docs.microsoft.com/en-us/azure/dns/delegate-subdomain

309. **Answer:** B

Explanation: The search operator offers an encounter with multiple tables and columns.

As for the syntax:

Table_name | search "search term."

Note: This topic appears in various forms on the test. There are three suitable responses to the query:

1. search in (Event) "error"
2. Event | search "error"
3. Event | where EventType == "error"

The following are some additional wrong response choices you might come across on the test:

1. Get-Event Event | where {$_.EventTye ג€"eq "error"}
2. Event | where EventType is "error"
3. select * from Event where EventType is "error"
4. search in (Event) * | where EventType ג€"eq "error"

For further details, you can visit the given URLs.

https://docs.microsoft.com/en-us/azure/azure-monitor/log-query/search-queries
https://docs.microsoft.com/en-us/azure/azure-monitor/log-query/get-started-portal https://docs.microsoft.com/en-us/azure/data-explorer/kusto/query/searchoperator?pivots=azuredataexplorer

310. **Answer:** D

Explanation: NS entries should be changed in the DNS domain registrar.

For further details, you can visit the given URL.

https://docs.microsoft.com/en-us/azure/dns/dns-delegate-domain-azure-dns

311. **Answer:** B

Explanation: Only each user's main username

For further details, you can visit the given URL.

https://docs.microsoft.com/en-us/azure/active-directory/enterprise-users/users-bulk-delete

IPSpecialist
Sharpen Your Skills for the Digital Future

About Our Products

Other products from IPSpecialist LTD regarding CSP technology are:

 AWS Certified Cloud Practitioner Study guide

 AWS Certified SysOps Admin - Associate Study guide

 AWS Certified Solution Architect - Associate Study guide

 AWS Certified Developer Associate Study guide

 AWS Certified Advanced Networking – Specialty Study guide

 AWS Certified Security – Specialty Study guide

 AWS Certified Big Data – Specialty Study guide

 AWS Certified Database – Specialty Study guide

 AWS Certified Machine Learning – Specialty Study guide

 Microsoft Certified: Azure Fundamentals

Microsoft Certified: Azure Administrator

Microsoft Certified: Azure Solution Architect

Microsoft Certified: Azure DevOps Engineer

Microsoft Certified: Azure Developer Associate

Microsoft Certified: Azure Security Engineer

Microsoft Certified: Azure Data Fundamentals

Microsoft Certified: Azure AI Fundamentals

Microsoft Certified: Azure Database Administrator Associate

Google Certified: Associate Cloud Engineer

Google Certified: Professional Cloud Developer

Microsoft Certified: Azure Data Engineer Associate

Microsoft Certified: Azure Data Scientist

Ansible Certified: Advanced Automation

Oracle Certified: OCI Foundations Associate

Oracle Certified: OCI Developer Associate

Oracle Certified: OCI Architect Associate

Oracle Certified: OCI Operations Associate

Kubernetes Certified: Application Developer

Other Network & Security related products from IPSpecialist LTD are:

- CCNA Routing & Switching Study Guide
- CCNA Security Second Edition Study Guide
- CCNA Service Provider Study Guide
- CCDA Study Guide
- CCDP Study Guide
- CCNP Route Study Guide
- CCNP Switch Study Guide
- CCNP Troubleshoot Study Guide
- CCNP Security SCOR Study Guide
- CCNP Service Provider SPCOR Study Guide
- CCNP Enterprise ENCOR Study Guide
- CCNP Enterprise ENARSI Study Guide

- CompTIA Network+ Study Guide
- CompTIA Security+ Study Guide
- Certified Blockchain Expert (CBEv2) Study Guide
- EC-Council CEH v10 Second Edition Study Guide
- EC-Council CEH v12 First Edition Study Guide
- Certified Blockchain Expert v2 Study Guide

Made in the USA
Middletown, DE
23 October 2023